CAMBRIDGE
UNIVERSITY PRESS

CAMBRIDGE
Global English

for Cambridge Primary English as a Second Language

Learner's Book 2

Elly Schottman & Caroline Linse

Series Editor: Kathryn Harper

Contents

Listening/Speaking	Cross-curricular links	Phonics/Word study	21st-century skills
Greet and introduce classmates Understand and repeat conversations Learn a TPR chant and months of the year song Ask/answer questions	**Maths:** Count from 1 to 30 Use calendar information (date, month) Enter and discuss information in a chart	Alphabet review Use a picture dictionary	Work together in partners and in groups Teach newly learned words to others **Critical thinking:** Ask for information and clarification Search for information online and in books (dictionary)
Listen for main ideas and details Follow instructions Ask and answer questions Discuss likes and dislikes Sing songs	**Language arts:** Distinguish between fiction and informational text Use a dictionary **Social studies:** Schools around the world **Maths:** Count Tell the time Understand information presented in a chart	Alphabet review; vowels and consonants Short vowel sounds Digraphs: sh, ch, tch, th Write words spelled aloud	Activate prior knowledge Work collaboratively, teamwork Search for information online on maps, in charts, in books Share ideas, information **Critical thinking:** Compare and contrast Classify Reflection / self-assessment **Values:** Being responsible
Listen for main idea and details Ask for, give and follow directions Listen to and conduct interviews Say, sing, act out poems and songs	**Geography:** Interpret a map, use a map grid Learn about countries and continents, landforms **Social studies:** Community, jobs	-r modified nouns: er, ar, ir, or, ur. Suffix: -er and -or Prefix: un-	Activate prior knowledge Work collaboratively Share ideas **Critical thinking:** Classify Enter information on maps, diagrams, survey charts Communicate information Reflection / self-assessment **Values:** Being a good global neighbour
Listen for details and main idea Follow and give instructions Recognise simple words spelled aloud Ask and answer questions Express likes, dislikes and feelings Play guessing games Say, sing, act out poems, song and play	**Science:** Parts of the body, healthy habits (food, exercise) Learn about diversity in birds Interpret a chart **PE:** Active games and challenges	Long vowel sounds and spelling: silent e Long a spellings: a_e, ai, ay Digraph: ph	Activate prior knowledge Work collaboratively Share ideas, information **Critical thinking:** Classify Compare and contrast Reflection / self-assessment **Values:** Identify feelings, show empathy
Listen for main idea and details Ask and answer questions Recall facts Describe actions and events, cause and effect Express feelings Say, sing and act out poems and songs	**Science:** Use physical models to learn about day and night, and how shadows change during the day Conduct shadow experiments Make predictions, record results and findings	Long i spellings: i_e, -ight, -y Compound words	Activate prior knowledge Work collaboratively Pose questions, research answers Share ideas, information **Critical thinking:** Cause and effect Make predictions Reflection / self-assessment **Values:** Wondering and learning about the world around us

Contents

Contents

Listening/Speaking	Cross-curricular links	Phonics/Word study	21st-century skills
Listen for main idea and details Ask and answer questions Follow instructions Express opinions Sing songs, say tongue twisters, act out stories	**Maths:** Counting to 100 by tens, forward and backward Counting by twos Estimating Measuring lengths with non-standard and standard units Geometric shapes	Words that sound alike (homophones)	Activate prior knowledge Do collaborative problem-solving Share ideas, information **Critical thinking:** Creative problem-solving State and support opinions Reflection / self-assessment **Values:** Identify character qualities we admire
Listen for main idea and details Ask and answer questions Spell words aloud Recall facts Discuss and describe animal appearance and behaviour Say, sing, act out poems, song, and stories	**Science:** Learn about insects and spiders Compare how animals are similar and different in their body parts Understand how insects help people	Rhyming words Long e spellings: ea, ee Variant sounds of ea: bread, tea	Work collaboratively Share ideas, information Activate prior knowledge Pose questions, research and answers **Critical thinking:** Compare and contrast Classify Cause and effect Sequence Reflection / self-assessment **Values:** Everyone needs a little help sometimes. It is important to be helpful.
Listen for main idea and details Follow and give instructions Ask and answer questions Discuss and apply information	**Science:** Environmental awareness and protection Parts of a plant Materials and goods from a tree	Long o spellings: o_e, oa, oe, ow, o Variant sounds of ow: slow, cow	Integrate prior knowledge Work collaboratively Share ideas, information **Critical thinking:** Classify Cause and effect Sequence Reflection / self-assessment **Values:** We need to take care of planet Earth.
Listen for main idea and details Follow and give instructions Ask and answer questions Make decisions and choices Share information	**Social studies / Geography:** Homes around the world World places Climates **Science:** Playground physics (ramps) Making predictions Animal homes Building materials	Long u spellings: u_e, ue, oo, ew Variant sounds of oo: look, roof	Activate prior knowledge Work collaboratively Share ideas, information **Critical thinking:** Compare and contrast Classify Cause and effect Interpret diagrams Reflection / self-assessment **Values:** Recognise the benefits of working together
Listen for information Follow directions Ask and answer questions Make and explain choices Express opinions, likes and dislikes	**Geography / Social studies:** Maps Places in a city Transportation Schedules Digital literacy	Identify opposites -ly suffix (adverbs)	Apply prior knowledge Work collaboratively Share ideas, information **Critical thinking:** Compare and contrast Interpret maps and diagrams Support an opinion with reasons Reflection / self-assessment **Values:** Appreciate your home Describe specific things you love about your home

How to use this book

In this book you will find lots of different features to help your learning.

Find out what you are going to learn in the lesson. ⟶

> **We are going to...**
> * spell our names and introduce a friend.

Get started by thinking about a 'big question'. Look at a photo and talk about what you know. ⟶

> **Getting started**
> What can you say when you meet a new friend?
> Share your ideas.

Important words and their meanings. These words are included on wordlists in the Teacher's Resource. ⟶

book map calendar clock tablet

The key words include vocabulary from other subjects, instruction words and Academic English terms. ⟶

> **Key words**
> **title:** name of a book or story
> **author:** the writer

Tips you can use to help you with your learning. ⟶

> **Writing tip**
> If your teacher is a man, use the word **he**.
> If your teacher is a woman, use the word **she**.

Be a Language detective! Find out more about grammar. ⟶

> **Language detective**
> Say and write the missing word.
> The children **sing**.
> Marco **sing**s.
> The children **read**.
> Marco _____.

At the end of each unit, there is a choice of projects to work on together, using what you have learned. You might do some research or make something.

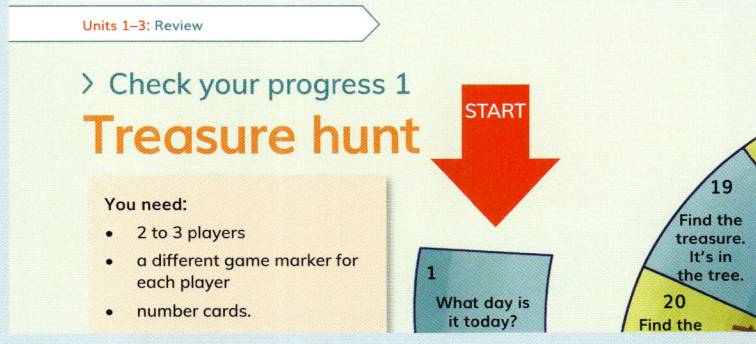

A: Make a survey

What's your favourite school subject?

Your teacher will give you a chart.

Read the subjects in the column on the left.

Ask your classmates, 'What's your favourite school subject?'

Ask them to write their names in the row next to that subject.

What's your favourite school subject?

Science					
Maths					
English					
Music					
Art					

Questions help you think about how you learn.

How did you help your group do the project?

Look at what you have learned in the unit! Think about which skills you do well and which you need more practice with.

Look what I can do!

- I can talk about classroom objects and school activities.
- I can talk about the time and the days of the week.
- I can talk about parts of a book.
- I can talk about who things belong to.
- I can read and write words with short vowel sounds.
- I can read and write about schools.

At the end of every 3 units, stop and check your progress! Play games and do activities to review what you have learned.

Units 1–3: Review

> Check your progress 1

Treasure hunt

START

You need:
- 2 to 3 players
- a different game marker for each player
- number cards.

1
What day is it today?

19
Find the treasure. It's in the tree.

20
Find the

Find out the meaning of words and stick your stickers in the Picture dictionary.

11 Food

apple	banana	bread
cake	carrot	cheese

bread

cheese

Audio is available with the Digital Learner's Book, the Teacher's Resource or Digital Classroom

Video is available with Digital Classroom

Lesson 1: The **Think About It** lesson introduces the topic through a big question and an image to generate discussion.

Many units include a video, available on Digital Classroom.

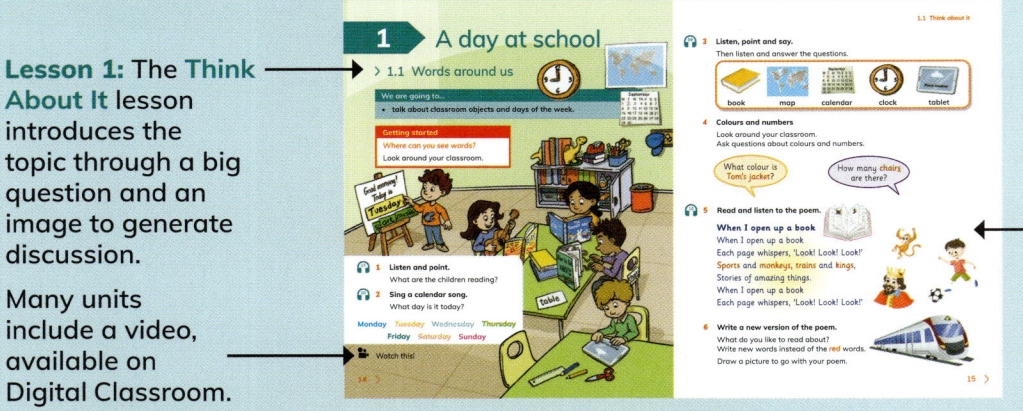

Poems and chants help to reinforce topic vocabulary.

Lesson 2: The **Let's Explore** lesson explores the unit topic further.

Sticker activities encourage learners to think critically.

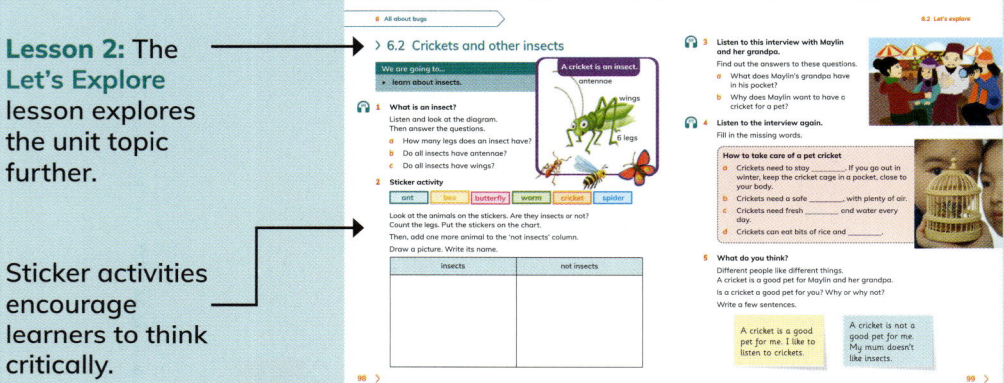

Lesson 3: The **cross-curricular** lesson prepares learners to learn in English across the curriculum.

In this lesson you'll find the key words.

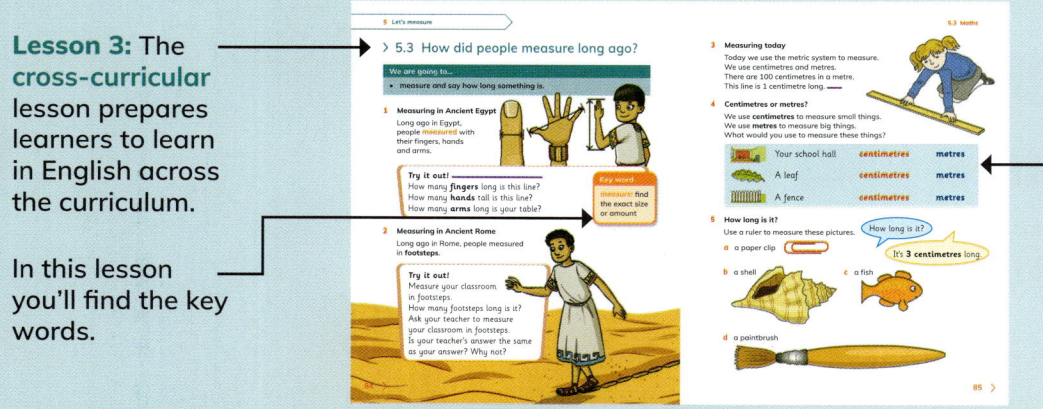

There are opportunities to think critically about the information in the text.

Lesson 4: The **Use of English** lesson develops grammar and language.

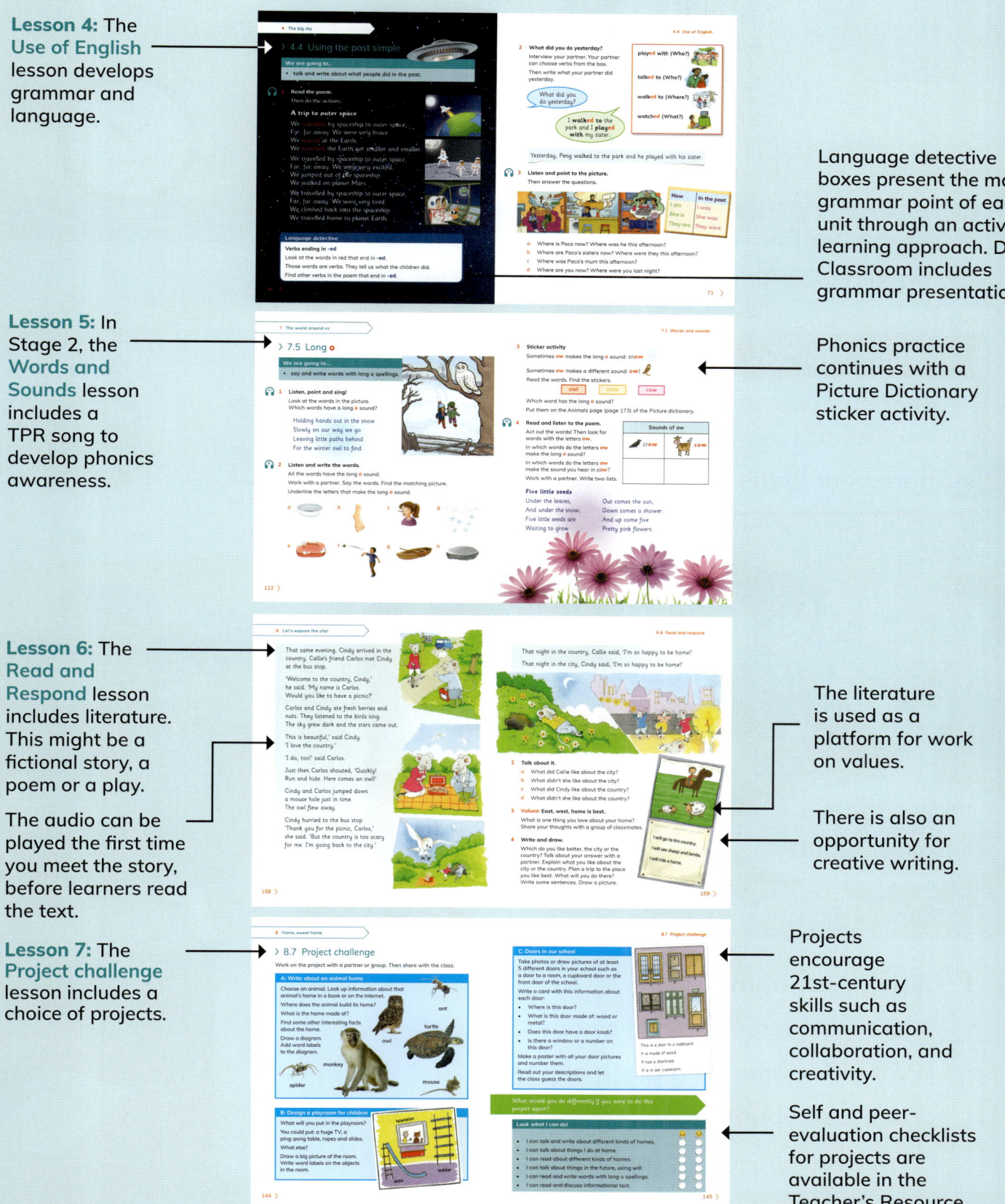

Language detective boxes present the main grammar point of each unit through an active learning approach. Digital Classroom includes grammar presentations.

Lesson 5: In Stage 2, the **Words and Sounds** lesson includes a TPR song to develop phonics awareness.

Phonics practice continues with a Picture Dictionary sticker activity.

Lesson 6: The **Read and Respond** lesson includes literature. This might be a fictional story, a poem or a play.

The audio can be played the first time you meet the story, before learners read the text.

The literature is used as a platform for work on values.

There is also an opportunity for creative writing.

Lesson 7: The **Project challenge** lesson includes a choice of projects.

Projects encourage 21st-century skills such as communication, collaboration, and creativity.

Self and peer-evaluation checklists for projects are available in the Teacher's Resource.

Starter unit

› 1 Welcome!

- spell our names and introduce a friend.

Getting started

What can you say when you meet a new friend?

Share your ideas.

He/His   She/Her

He is a boy   She is a girl
His name is...   Her name is...

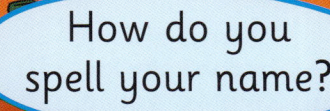

How do you spell your name?

This is my partner. Her name is Rani. She likes trees.

I like trees.

 01   **1   Spell your name.**

Listen to the boy spell his name.

Write his name on a piece of paper.

Then, ask your partner, *How do you spell your name?*

Write your partner's name.

 2 **What does Rani like?**

Listen to Amara introduce her partner, Rani.

Does Amara say **She** or **He**? Why?

Language tip

Look at the chart on the wall in the big picture.

3 **Talk with your class about things you like.**

Make a list.

Then draw a picture and write a sentence below: *I like ...*

Things we like

ice cream   football   flowers

 4 **Introduce your partner.**

Listen to Amara introduce Rani again. Then introduce your partner.

First, write the sentences.

Then tell the class your partner's name and what he or she likes.

 5 **Learn a hello and goodbye chant.**

Bread and butter, honey and jam
Say hello as **quickly** as you can.

Bread and butter, honey and jam
Say goodbye as **softly** as you can.

〉 2 The calendar

We are going to...

- **talk about the dates and months of the year.**

1 Count the days.

Look at the calendar for the month of September.

There are 30 days in September.

Point to the numbers as you count.

 2 Find the date.

Listen, repeat and point to these dates on the calendar.

1st September	**2nd September**	**3rd September**	**5th September**
9th September	**16th September**	**23rd September**	**30th September**

 3 Twelve months in a year.

Listen and point to the names of the months as you sing.

4 **Look at the birthday chart.**

Answer these questions. Then think of your own questions.

a   How many children have birthdays in April? When is Kira's birthday?

b   Look at October. When is Sami's birthday?

c   Which month has the most birthdays?

5 **When is your birthday?**

Make a birthday chart with your class.
Ask and answer questions.

6 **Listen and match.**

What can you say when you don't understand a word in English?

Listen and repeat. Point to the correct picture in Activity 7.

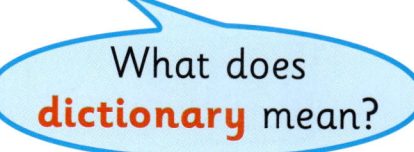
What does **dictionary** mean?

What's a **mobile phone**?

7 **How do you say it in English?**

Think of a word that you would like to say in English.

Look it up! Practise saying it!

Use a computer , a mobile phone or a dictionary .

Write the word and draw a picture.

Teach your new word to your class.

How do you say in English?

Volcano.

1 ▶ A day at school

> 1.1 Words around us

We are going to...

- talk about classroom objects and days of the week.

Getting started

Where can you see words?

Look around your classroom.

 1 **Listen and point.**

What are the children reading?

 2 **Sing a calendar song.**

What day is it today?

Monday **Tuesday** **Wednesday** **Thursday**

Friday **Saturday** **Sunday**

 Watch this!

3 **Listen, point and say.**

Then listen and answer the questions.

| book | map | calendar | clock | tablet |

4 **Colours and numbers**

Look around your classroom.
Ask questions about colours and numbers.

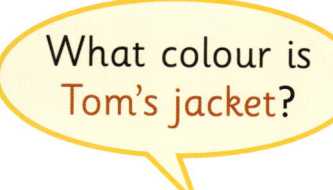

What colour is Tom's jacket?

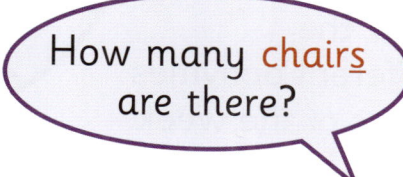

How many chairs are there?

 5 **Read and listen to the poem.**

When I open up a book

When I open up a book
Each page whispers, 'Look! Look! Look!'
Sports and monkeys, trains and kings,
Stories of amazing things.
When I open up a book
Each page whispers, 'Look! Look! Look!'

6 **Write a new version of the poem.**

What do you like to read about?
Write new words instead of the red words.

Draw a picture to go with your poem.

> 1.2 Our busy classroom

We are going to...

- talk about time, days of the week and school activities.

1   What time is it?

Use a paper clip on the clock to show a time. Ask your partner: "What time is it?"

 2   Sticker activity

In Marco's class, the children do different activities on different days of the week.

Listen to Marco and put stickers on the chart.

It's three o'clock.

Monday	Tuesday	Wednesday	Thursday	Friday

What does Marco do on **Tuesday**?

He sings.

Language detective

Say and write the missing word.

The children **sing**.
Marco **sings**.

The children **read**.
Marco _____.

3 **Real or make-believe?**

There are a lot of books in Marco's classroom.
Some of the books tell stories.
Stories are not real; they are make-believe.
The people or animals in a story are
called **characters**.
Look at the book, *The Snowy Day*.
Who are the characters?

Some books give real information.
Look at the book, *Animals in the Winter*.
Do you think it tells a story or gives real information?
Why do you think so?

4 **Choose some books.**

Different children like
different kinds of books.
Choose books for Rasha
and Miguel. Then choose
a book for yourself!

My name is Rasha.
I like reading books with my dad.
We like learning new things.

My name is Miguel.
I like funny stories about
animals. I don't like scary
stories!

5 **Draw and write: A book for me!**

Draw the cover of a book you would like to read.
Does your book tell a story or give real information?
Write the name of the book on the cover.

> 1.3 Inside a book

We are going to...

- **talk about parts of a book.**

1   Look at the cover of a book.

What is the **title** of the book?
Who is the **author** of the book?
Find another book in your classroom.
Answer the questions again.

Schools Around the World
Mateo Diaz

2   Look inside a book.

A contents page is at the beginning of a book. It tells you what is in the book. There are four chapters in this book.

Here are four pictures from the book *Schools Around the World*. In which chapter can you find each picture? Which page will you look at?

Contents   page

1 School uniforms   2
2 First day of school 6
3 Art class   10
4 Lunchtime   14

a These children in China are painting in art class. Li Na stands up to show her picture.

b These boys eat lunch in their classroom in Oman.

c Sizani and Nandi live in South Africa. All the children in their class wear green school jackets.

d Ivan lives in Russia. On the first day of school, Ivan and his friends bring flowers for their teacher.

3 **Compare and contrast.**

Think about how your own school is similar to and different from the schools described in *Schools Around the World*. Talk with a partner or your class.

a Do you have art class in your school? What do you use to make art?

☐ Crayons? ☐ Markers? ☐ Paint? ☐ Clay?

b Do you eat lunch at your school? Where do you eat lunch?

☐ At home ☐ In our classroom
☐ In our school cafeteria ☐ Outdoors at school

c Do you wear uniforms in your school? Describe what you are wearing now.

d What do you do on the first day of school?

How do you say the name of your country in English?

> 1.4 Talking about possessions

We are going to...

- talk about who things belong to.

1 Whose backpack is it?

Look at the picture. These children are on a field trip and their backpacks are all mixed up!

Listen and repeat. Draw a line with your finger from the child to his or her backpack.

Jill Jing Jack Lucy

Say and write the name of the child. Remember to use **'s**.

Lucy**'s** backpack is red.

_____ backpack is blue with white stars.

_____ backpack is yellow with orange stripes.

_____ backpack is black.

Language detective

Look at different ways of talking about possessions.

Is this **your backpack?** = Is it **yours**?
Yes, it's **my backpack**. = Yes, it's ____.
Which **backpack?** = Which **one**?
The red **backpack**. = The red ____.

2 **What do they have in their backpacks?**

Talk with your partner.
This is Jill's backpack.
What does she have in her backpack?

This is Jing's backpack.
What does he have in his backpack?

He has two keys.

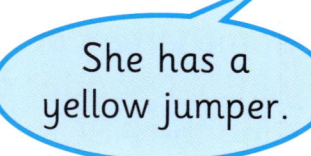

She has a yellow jumper.

ball	skipping rope	phone	jumper	pencil

lunchbox	notebook	sunglasses	hat	key

3 **Can you remember?**

Choose one of the backpacks in Activity 2. Is it Jill's or Jing's?

Look at the picture of the things inside. Then close your eyes.

Tell your partner what is in the backpack.

Win a point for each thing you remember!

Who has the most points?

> 1.5 Review of short vowels

We are going to...

- **read and write words with short vowel sounds.**

 1 Sing an ABC song. ♪♫♪♪

Point to the letters as you sing.

A B C D E F G H I J
K L M N O P Q R S T
U V W X Y Z

2 Clap the vowels.

Some letters are called **consonants** and some are called **vowels**.
A, E, I, O, and U are vowels.
Sing the ABC song again. Clap when you sing each vowel.

 3 Sticker activity
These words start with the 5 short vowel sounds.
Listen, point and say. Then put the stickers on the
Alphabet chart (page 165).

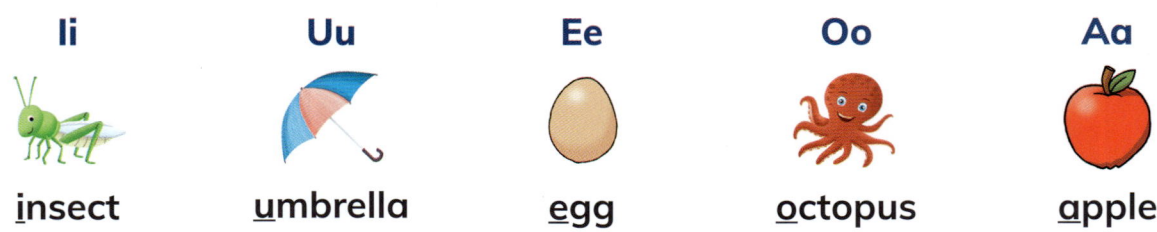

Ii	Uu	Ee	Oo	Aa
insect	umbrella	egg	octopus	apple

 4 Find the vowels in the middle.

Write the 5 vowel letters on 5 cards. Listen and repeat these words.

Which vowel sound do you hear in the middle? Hold up the card.

1   2   3   4   5

Say a sentence for each picture.

5 **Look and say the sounds of sh, ch, th, and tch.**

Look for these letter combinations in some of the pictures below.
Say the words.

What special sound does each letter combination make?

cat	catch	cut	maths	pen
chips	ship	shop	rock	fifth

6 **Play a partner game: How do you spell it?**

Choose a picture from Activity 5.

Your partner will ask, 'How do you spell it?'

Your partner will write down the letters,
say the word and point to the picture.

How do you spell it?

p-e-n.

7 **Make a bilingual word poster.**

Work with a group. Think of
a category, for example,
toys, **animals** or **food**.

Find photos or draw pictures
of things in that category.

Write the words in your
home language and
in English.

Toys

la muñeca
a doll

el patinete
a scooter

la pelota
a ball

> 1.6 My school

We are going to...

- **read and write about schools.**

1 Before you read

This reading has 5 chapters.
Each chapter title is written in **blue letters**.
Read the titles then look at the pictures.
What do you think each chapter is about?

 ## My school

Chapter 1: This is my school

My name is Fernando.
I live in Cebu, the Philippines.
I go to Oceanside Primary School.
I am in the second grade.
My teacher's name is Ms Cruz.

Chapter 2: My classroom

In my classroom there are tables and chairs.
There are windows with curtains.
There is a world map and a calendar on the wall.
My teacher puts our artwork on the board.
The room looks cheerful and bright!

Chapter 3: Science class

I like science class. We study electricity.
We do experiments. Our teacher tells
us safety rules.
We listen and follow the rules.
We use batteries and wires to make
a light bulb turn on.

Chapter 4: Break time

I have 15 minutes for break time.
I go outside for break time.
I have a snack. I eat dried mango.
When the bell rings I know break
time is over.

Chapter 5: End of the day

It's almost 2:00. I tidy up my desk.
I put my homework in my backpack.
I put on my jacket and line up at the door.
It's time to go home!

2   Compare and contrast.

Look at the sentences and the picture in each chapter.

a   How is your **classroom** the same as Fernando's? How is it different?

b   How is your **science class** and Fernando's science class the same or different?

c   How is **break time** at your school and Fernando's school the same or different?

d   What do you do at the end of the school day? What do you do that is the same as Fernando? What do you do that is different?

3   Values: What does being responsible mean?

✓   You take good care of your books and papers.

✓   You use science materials carefully and safely.

✓   You tidy up after yourself.

✓   You remember to do your homework.

What does Fernando do that shows he is **responsible**?

What do you do that shows you are **responsible**?

Be responsible

4 **Write a class book.**

You are going to write a book with your class called **'This is our school'**.

Follow these steps to write your book.

Step 1: Plan with your class.	• What chapters will you have in your book? • Make a list. You can use the chapter titles in Fernando's book. • You can think of other chapter titles too.
Step 2: Work with a group to write a chapter.	• Each group will write a different chapter. • Use the questions in Activity 1 and questions your teacher gives you to help you write.
Step 3: Check your work.	• After you write your chapter, read your sentences aloud. • Did you remember to write all the words?
Step 4: Draw a picture.	• Draw a picture to go with your sentences.
Step 5: Make a cover for your book.	• Write the title and authors on the cover. Add a picture.

Writing tip

Fernando wrote his book by himself so he uses the words *I* and *my*.

I am in the second grade.
My teacher's name is Ms Cruz.

You are writing your chapter with other children, so you will use the words *we* and *our*.

We are in the second grade.
Our teacher's name is...

Does your school have a **website**?
Look at the website to find photos or facts you can use in your book.

> 1.7 Project challenge

Work on the project with a partner or group.
Then share with the class.

A: Make a survey

What's your favourite school subject?

Your teacher will give you a chart.

Read the subjects in the column on the left.

Ask your classmates, 'What's your favourite school subject?'

Ask them to write their names in the row next to that subject.

What's your favourite school subject?					
Science					
Maths					
English					
Music					
Art					

B: Make word cards for your classroom

Write the names of things in your classrooms on cards.

(Look in the Picture dictionary on page 169 for some words and ideas.)

Stick each word card on or near the object.

Teach the words to your class.

Say 'Point to the **clock**, please!'

C: Introduce your partner

Ask your partner questions. Write down the answers.

Then introduce your partner to the class.

- What's your name?
- How do you spell your name?
- How old are you?
- What colours do you like?
- Do you have any brothers or sisters?

This is my partner.
_____ name is _____.
_____ is _____ years old.
_____ likes the colours _____ and _____.
_____ has _____ brothers and _____ sisters.

How did you help your group do the project?

Look what I can do!

- I can talk about classroom objects and school activities.
- I can talk about the time and the days of the week.
- I can talk about parts of a book.
- I can talk about who things belong to.
- I can read and write words with short vowel sounds.
- I can read and write about schools.

2 Good neighbours

> 2.1 People in your neighbourhood

We are going to...

- talk about workers in our neighbourhood.

Getting started

Who lives and works in your neighbourhood?

1 **Listen and point.**

Ben and his family are helping their neighbours.

What is Ben doing?
What is his cousin doing?

What are his sister and grandpa doing?

2 **Listen, point and say.**

window cleaner   police officer   reporter   nurse   bus driver

3 **Look at the big picture.**

Then answer the questions.

What is the police officer doing?

Who is the nurse helping?

Work with a partner.
Ask other questions that begin with **What**? and **Who**?

4 **Count the people in the big picture.**

How many children? How many grown-ups?
How many people all together?

 5 **Read and say the poem.**

My neighbourhood

Come and meet the people in my neighbourhood.

There are neighbours helping neighbours in my neighbourhood.

There are grandmas, grandpas, cousins,

Mums and dads, girls and boys,

In my neighbourhood, the streets around my home.

› 2.2 Jobs

We are going to...

- **learn about different jobs.**

20

1 **Read and listen.**

Use stickers to label the firefighters' clothes in the picture.

> Firefighters have important jobs. They put out fires.
>
> They rescue people who are inside burning buildings.
>
> Firefighters wear special clothes that keep them safe.
>
> They wear heavy **boots** on their feet.
>
> They wear heavy **jackets** made from materials that do not burn.
>
> Firefighters wear **helmets**. If something falls on a firefighter's head, the helmet keeps the firefighter safe.
>
> A firefighter wears a **mask** on their face and an air pack on their back. The mask lets the firefighter breathe fresh air.
>
> Firefighters wear heavy **gloves** on their hands.
> They can touch hot things with their gloves.

2 **Listen to an interview.**

Josef is a year 2 student.
He is interviewing a firefighter.

The firefighter's name is Miss Dilov.

Listen to the interview to learn about
Miss Dilov's job.

Look at the picture here and on page 32.
Point to some of the things Miss Dilov
talks about.

3 **Complete the report.**

Josef writes a report about Miss Dilov and her job.
Fill in the missing words.

> Miss Dilov ____*is*____ a firefighter.
> ____*She*____ _____ at the fire station.
> When there's a fire, she _____ on the fire engine.
> She uses _____ to fight the fire.
> She also visits _____ and _____ to children about fire safety.

4 **Interview your teacher.**

A teacher has an important job.
Imagine you are a reporter.

Interview your teacher.
Use these questions.

- What is your job?
- Where do you work?
- What do you teach?

5 **Write a report.**

Write a report about your teacher's job.
Look at Josef's report for ideas.

Writing tip

If your teacher is a man,
use the word **he**.

If your teacher is a woman,
use the word **she**.

> 2.3 Where do you live?

We are going to...

- **talk about where we live.**

1 **Read the letter and talk about the questions.**

This is a letter from Silvia.

Dear unknown friend,

My name is Silvia Lopez. I am eight years old.
I live in an apartment building. My family lives on
the second floor. Look at the picture I drew of my
building. Can you see me?

I live in Mexico, in a city called Merida. On the map,
Merida is in square D-1. Can you see it?

My grandparents live in the largest city in Mexico.
It is the capital of Mexico. It
is in square C-1 of the map.
Can you find the name of
the city?

What is the capital of your
country? Do you live in the
capital?

I like to travel and meet new
friends. Maybe someday you
and I will meet!

Your friend,

Silvia

2   **Learn about continents.**

Silvia lives in Mexico. Mexico is in North America.

North America is a **continent**.

How many continents are there?

Which one do you live in?

Key word

continent: Africa is a continent

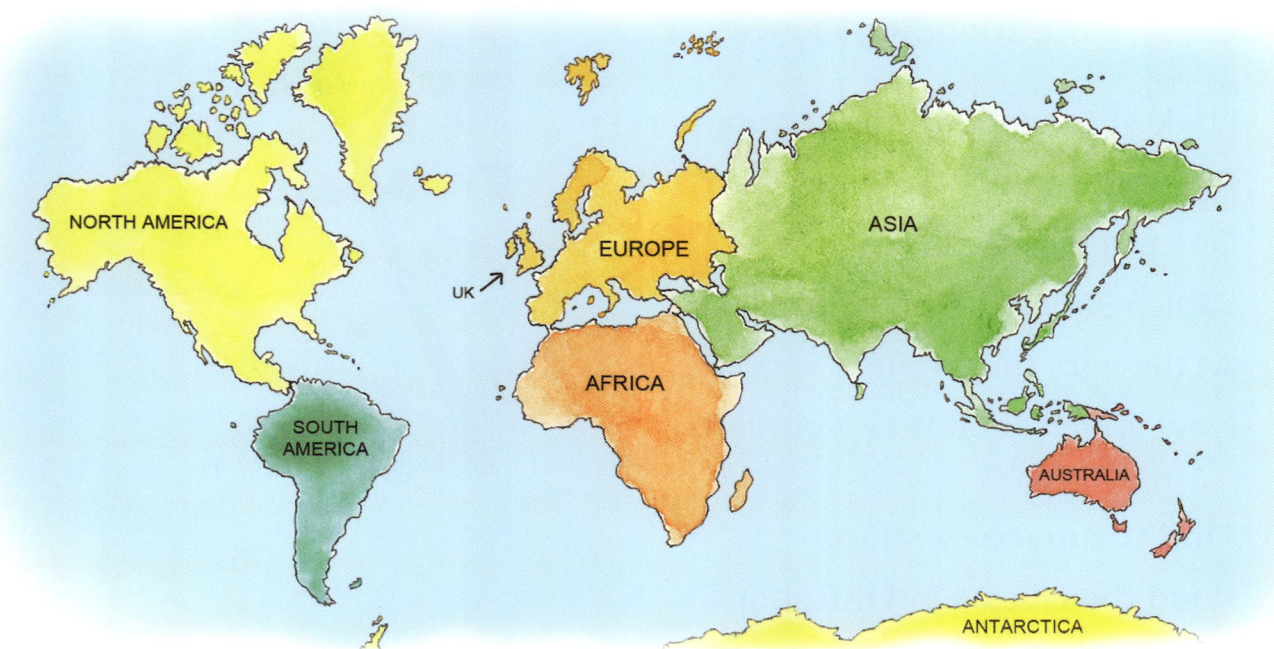

3   **In the lift: Going up!**

Silvia's grandparents live in a tall apartment building. Silvia likes pressing the buttons in the lift. Which button does she press to get to each floor?

third floor	3
twelfth floor	_____
tenth floor	_____
second floor	_____
fourteenth floor	_____
first floor	_____

> 2.4 Saying where things are

We are going to...

- **ask for and give directions.**

1 Explore the shopping centre.

Look at the map of the shopping centre.

Put your finger on the **red** star.

Go straight ahead.

Which shops are on your left?

At the end, turn right.

Now which shop is on your left?

2 Find the mystery shop.

Read the clues. Find the shops.

1 It's between the bookshop and the sweet shop.

2 It's next to the shoe shop.

3 It's opposite the gift shop.

Write a new clue. Read it aloud. Can your friends find it?

Language detective

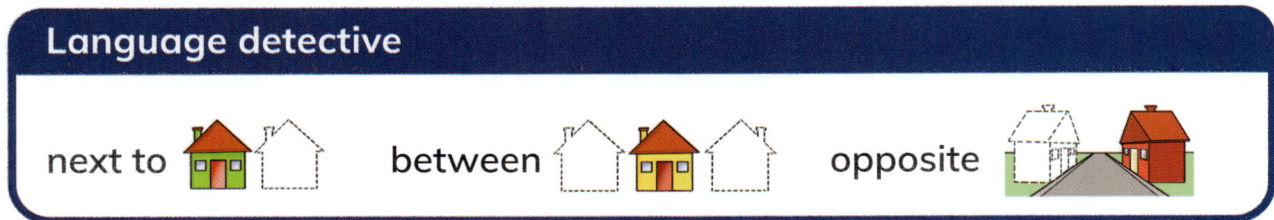

next to   between   opposite

3 Ask for directions.

Listen and follow the directions.
Practise the conversation with a partner.

Excuse me, where is the gift shop?

4 Look at the pictures.

Then listen and follow the instructions.

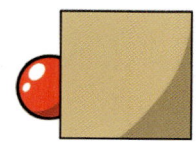            

behind   **in front of**   **in**   **on**   **under**

 5 Find the treasure.

Two children are on a treasure hunt. Listen to each clue.

Where do the children look? Where is the treasure?

6 Make up a clue.

Say a clue for your partner.
Your partner must point to the map.

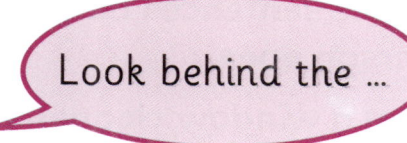

7 Classroom treasure hunt

Work in a group. Write four clues for your classroom.

Then hide clues 2, 3 and 4. Put a treasure where clue 4 says the treasure is. Give clue 1 to another group!

Here are some examples.

1 Look in front of the crayons.   2 Look under the teacher's chair.   3 Look in a red book.   4 Look behind the door.

Clue 4 leads to the treasure! Where did these children put the treasure?

❯ 2.5 Vowels followed by r

We are going to...

- **read and write words with -er, -ir, -or, -ur.**

 1 **Jobs that end in -er and -or**

Listen and repeat the sentences.
Listen to the sound that **-er** and **-or** makes.

a I'm a **singer**. I sing.

sing + **er** = sing**er**

b I'm a **teacher**. I teach.

teach + **er** = teach**er**

c I'm an **actor**. I act.

act + **or** = act**or**

Would you like to be a singer, a teacher, or an actor?

2 **Finish the sentences below by saying what the person does.**

a I am a **window cleaner**. I ___clean___ windows.

b I am a **writer**. I _____ books.

c I am a **sailor**. I _____ boats.

d I am a **painter**. I _____ pictures.

e I am a **clothes designer**. I _____ clothes.

f I am a **baker**. I _____ bread.

3 **Who am I?**

Act out a worker at work. Your friends ask questions to guess your job.

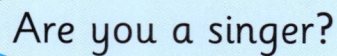

Are you a singer?

No, I'm not. Try again.

4 Read the sentences.

Look and listen for the sounds of vowels followed by r.

Find the matching picture.

a   I am a sailor. I got a sailboat for my birthday.

b   I am a birdwatcher. I like to watch birds.

c   I'm a writer. This is a story about a tiger.

d   I am a nurse. Does your elbow hurt?

Language tip

The spellings **-er**, **-ir**, **-or** and **-ur** can all stand for the same sound!

Write the words in Activity 4 that have the spelling **-er**, **-ir**, **-or** or **-ur**.

1

2

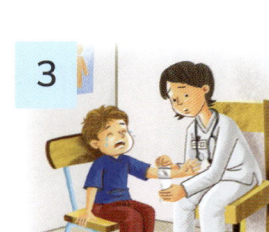

3

4

5 Sticker activity

| baker | actor | painter | doctor | nurse |

Read the words. Look for the spellings **er**, **or**, and **ur**. Put the matching stickers on the Jobs page (page 172) of the Picture dictionary.

6 Listen and sing.

Point to the picture of each job mentioned in the song. When you grow up, what do you want to be?

Lots of jobs

Look around at all the jobs.
There's lots of work to do.
What do you want to be?
The choice is up to you.

› 2.6 A lot of kids

We are going to…

- read and talk about a poem and a song.

1   Before you read

The title of this poem is A *lot of kids*. Look quickly over the lines of the poem.
How many times can you find the phrase **a lot of**?
How many times can you find the words **kids** and **kid**?

A lot of kids

There are a lot of kids

Living in my apartment building

And a lot of apartment buildings on my street

And a lot of streets in this city

And cities in this country

And a lot of countries in the world.

So I wonder if somewhere there's a kid I've never met
Living in some building on some street
In some city and country, I'll never know –
And I wonder if that kid and I might be best friends
If we ever met.

Jeff Moss

2   Talk about the poem.

a   Where does the girl in this poem live?

b   Are there many apartment buildings on her street?

c   Do you think that the girl is **friendly** or **unfriendly**?

d   Do you think this poem is **happy** or **unhappy**?

Language detective

What is the meaning of **un-** at the beginning of a word?

helpful   **un**helpful

Can you think of another word for **sad** that begins with **un-**?

---

3   Write a letter to an unknown friend.

Tell the friend your name, where you live and what you like to do.

Look at the letter from Silvia on page 34.
You can begin and end your letter the way she does:

Dear unknown friend,
my name is Diego.
I live in San José.
San José is in Costa Rica.
I like to run and play with my
friends. May be we can meet
someday.
Your friend,
Diego

4 **Values:** Taking care of Planet Earth

The people who live on our street are our neighbours.
People who live in other countries are also our neighbours.
We all need to work together to take care of Planet Earth.

Listen and join in the song.

We've got the whole world in our hands

Chorus We've got the whole world in our hands. (sing 4 times)

We've got our brothers and our sisters in our hands,
We've got our friends and our family in our hands,
We've got people everywhere in our hands,
We've got the whole world in our hands.

We've got the sun and the rain
in our hands,
We've got the moon and the stars
in our hands,
We've got the wind and the clouds
in our hands,
We've got the whole world in our hands.

We've got the rivers and the mountains
in our hands,
We've got the seas and the oceans in our hands,
We've got the towns and the cities in our hands,
We've got the whole world in our hands.

 Watch this!

> 2.7 Project challenge

Work on the project with a partner or group.

Then share with the class.

A: Do a survey

What do you want to be?

- Make a chart. Choose 4 interesting jobs.

- Ask your classmates: What do you want to be when you grow up?

- Write their names on the chart.

Look at the sample chart.
Which job is the most popular?

Job	Names			
painter	Sam	Vijay	Maya	Franco
pilot	Elsa	Seth	Basil	
clothes designer	Lisa	Amir	Layla	
doctor	Leon			

B: Special clothes for special jobs

What special clothes do a **beekeeper**, a **hockey player** and a **sea diver** wear?

- Choose one job. Draw a picture of a person wearing the clothes.

- Write word labels for some of the clothes.

- Discuss how special clothes keep the person safe.

- Look in books and on the computer for more information.

C: Draw a school map

- Draw a map of the rooms in your school.
- Label the rooms. Add a photo of your classroom, if you like.
- A visitor comes to your school.
- Put your finger on the red star.
- Tell the visitor how to get to your classroom, the office, the toilets.

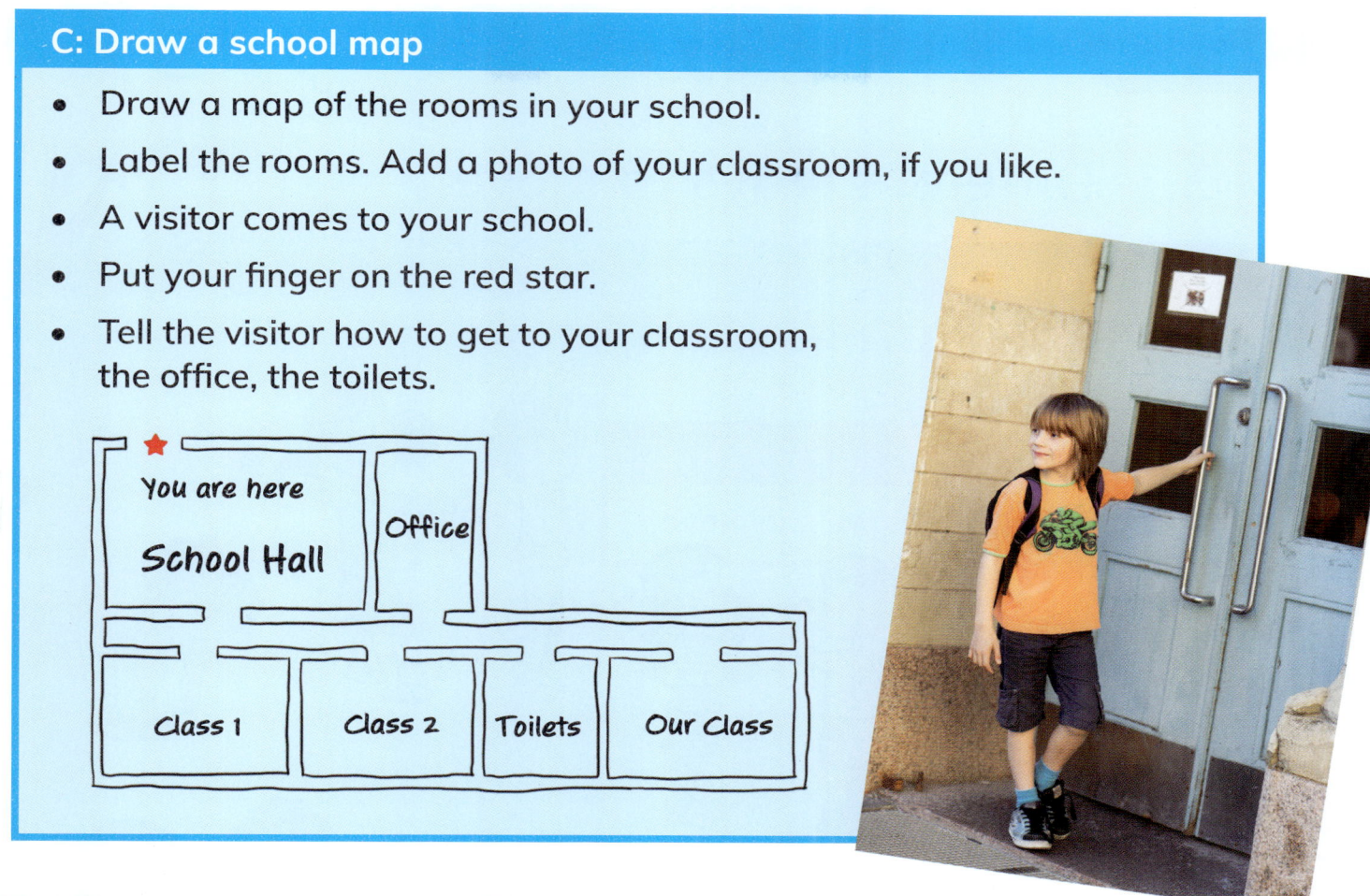

What is something new you learned from this project?

Look what I can do!

- I can talk about workers in my neighbourhood.
- I can learn about different jobs.
- I can talk about where I live.
- I can ask for and give directions.
- I can read and write words with -ar, -er, -ir, -or, -ur.
- I can read and talk about a poem and a song.

3 ▸ Ready, steady, go!

› 3.1 Different ways to move

We are going to...

- talk about ways we can move.

Getting started

What are some ways we can move?

Wave your hands.

Hop on one foot.

Nod your head.

 1 **Listen to Julia talk about 'Get up and move' day.**

What are the children doing?

Can you wave your hands, hop on one foot and nod your head?

2 **Listen, say and do.**

wave   stand   hop   fall   flap   wiggle   nod

Can you do each action?

3 **Read and point.**

Read the word labels and point to the parts of the boy's body.

What other 'parts of the body' words do you know?

Take turns giving instructions to your class: **Touch your ...**

 4 **Listen and read.**

Do the actions as you say the poem. Then look at the pictures opposite.

Find the children who are doing each action.

Reach for the sky!

Clap your hands, touch your toes.

Turn around. Put your finger on your nose.

Flap your arms, jump up high.

Wiggle your fingers and reach for the sky!

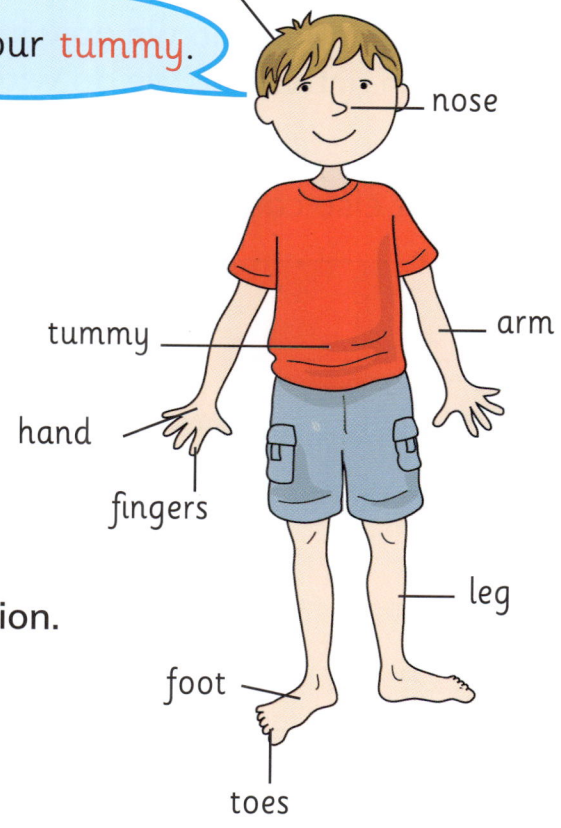

Touch your tummy.

head
nose
tummy
arm
hand
fingers
leg
foot
toes

Reading tip

Look at the body diagram in the Picture dictionary, on page 167.

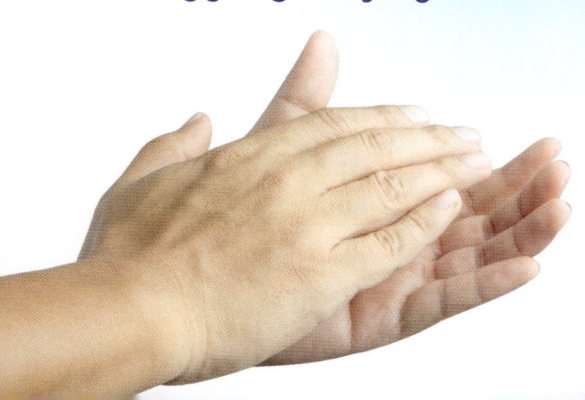

> 3.2 Healthy and strong

We are going to...

- **talk about ways we can move**

1 Sticker activity

Which actions do we do with our feet?
Which actions do we do with our hands?

Sort the stickers into the chart.

What else can we do with our hands and feet?

hands	feet

2 Write it, read it, do it.

Write three sentences. Use one word or phrase from each box.
Read the sentences to your partner.

Can your partner do all 3 actions at the same time?

| Clap Wave Shake | your hands. | Tap Hop on Stand on | one foot. | Nod Shake Roll | your head. |

3   Choose and write.

Walking, running and cycling are all great ways to keep your body strong. Eating healthy foods is also important.

Choose 3 activities and 3 healthy foods that you like.

I like...		
activities		
1		
2		
3		
food		
1		
2		
3		

Is there an activity or a food that you like, and your partner likes too?

Is there an activity or a food that your partner likes but you don't like?

My partner **and** I like _____.

My partner likes _____, **but** I don't.

Language tip

We can count apples, so we say:
apples or **3 apples** or **some apples**.

We can't count milk so we say:
milk or **some milk** (NOT ~~some milks~~)

 35

4   Balance on one foot!

Try it! Which foot did you stand on – your left foot or your right foot?

Which foot did most children in the class choose? Listen and follow the instructions.

> 3.3 What can birds do?

We are going to…

- read and talk about birds and what they can do.

1   Before you read.

Think about this question: *Can all birds fly?* Look at the **headings**. Where will you find the answer?

2   Amazing birds

Laying eggs
All birds have feathers and all birds lay eggs.
A hummingbird has the smallest egg.
It is as small as your fingernail.
An ostrich has the biggest egg. It is as big as 24 hen's eggs.

An ostrich and her eggs

Building nests
Most birds build nests for their eggs, but **some** birds don't.
Emperor penguins don't build nests. The father penguin balances the egg on his feet.
His tummy keeps the egg warm.
Some birds lay their eggs on the ground.

An Emperor penguin dad keeps the egg warm.

Flying
Most birds can fly, but some birds can't.
An ostrich can't fly, but it can run very fast.
A penguin can't fly, but it can swim very fast.

Swimming
Ducks and swans can swim. They can fly too!

Swans

3   **Talk about it.**

What new facts did you learn?
Which of the birds live near you?

4   **Complete the sentences.**

Look back at the text about amazing birds.
Find the words **all**, **most** and **some**.

Read the sentences aloud. Then finish
these sentences. How many different
sentences can you make?

All birds _____.
Most birds _____.
Some birds _____.

Key words

all

most

some

5   **What can birds do?**

Say what the birds below **can** and **can't** do.
Write a sentence about each bird.

	fly	swim	walk
kiwi			✓
hummingbird	✓		
goose	✓	✓	✓
falcon	✓		✓

Language focus

and   but   or

I can run **and** jump.

I can walk, **but** I can't fly.

A bird can't read **or** ride
a bike.

A kiwi can't fly **or**
swim, **but** it can walk.

kiwi

hummingbird

goose

falcon

51

> 3.4 Describing ongoing actions

We are going to...

- talk about what people are doing.

1   What can you do with a piece of paper?

Read each sentence and act it out.
Pretend you have a piece of paper in your hands.

I'm waving it.

You're ripping it.

He's cutting it.

She's folding it.

We're writing on it.

They're using paper in different ways.

2   Listen and guess.

You will need a piece of paper.
Sit back to back with your partner.

Partner A: Do something with a piece of paper, for example cut it, fold it or rip it.

Partner B: Listen carefully. Guess what your partner is doing.

Partner A

Partner B

Are you cutting the paper?

No, I'm not. Try again.

Language detective

These verbs are from Activity 1. They end in silent **e**:

wav**e**   writ**e**

Look carefully. When we add **-ing**, which letter disappears?

These verbs end in one vowel + one consonant:

rip   cut

Look for these verbs in Activity 1.
What happens to the final consonant when we add **-ing**?

3 **School field day**

Write the **-ing** form of these verbs.
Then listen and point to each action in the picture.

kick   climb   balance   win   run   hop

4 **Guess the mystery boy.**

Listen and find the mystery boy in the picture above.
Then play the game with your class.

5 **Write a clue.**

Write a description of one boy in the picture. Give it to your partner.
Can your partner find the boy?

He is wearing a yellow t-shirt. He is climbing the climbing wall.

> 3.5 Long vowel sounds

We are going to...

- **read and write words with long vowel sounds.**

 1 Which vowel sound?

A long vowel sound says the name of the vowel: **a e i o u**

Write the vowels **a**, **i** and **o** on three pieces of paper.
Listen for the sound in the middle of these words.

Hold up the vowel sound you hear.

a b c d e f

 2 Listen and say the word pairs.

How does the silent **e** change the
sound of the vowel?

| Tim | time |
| Sam | same |

3 Write the words.

Work with a partner. Write the
words for the six pictures in Activity 1.

All the words end in a silent **e**.

4 Read and find words with the long a sound.

Write the words. Draw a line under the letters that
stand for the long a sound: **a-e**, **ai** or **ay**.

On rainy days, the snails come out to play.
We can sail away to a place on the bay.

5   **Sticker activity**

playground   teacher   glue   slide

Read the words. Find the matching stickers.
What long vowel sound do you hear in each word?

Put the stickers on the School page (page 169) of the Picture dictionary.

 6   **Look at the photos.**

Listen and say what each child is feeling.
Act out a word for your partner to guess.

scared   tired   unhappy   angry   confused   excited

Are you feeling scared?

No, I'm not. Try again!

 7   **Listen, sing and do the actions.**

If you're happy and you know it

If you're **happy** and you know it, **clap your hands**.

If you're **happy** and you know it, **clap** your hands.

If you're **happy** and you know it,

And you really want to show it,

If you're **happy** and you know it, **clap** your hands.

⟩ 3.6 Bear and Turtle have a race

We are going to...

- read, talk about and act out a play.

1   Before you read

Look at the pictures and the names written in **purple**. Who are the characters in this play?

Reading tip

This folktale is from the Seneca Indians in the United States.

Bear and Turtle have a race

Narrator: One cold winter day,
              Bear is walking and singing.

Bear: *I'm the best in the forest.*
          I'm the fastest runner of all.
          I'm big and fast and strong and brave!
          I'm better than you all.

Turtle 1: Bear is always boasting.

Turtle 2: Bear makes me angry!

Turtle 3: I think we need to teach him a lesson.

Narrator: The turtles whisper together. They have a plan.

Turtle 2: Good idea!

Turtle 3: Very clever.

Turtle 4: Let's do it!

Narrator: The next day, Bear sees Turtle sitting on a rock.

Bear: What are you doing, Turtle?

Turtle 1: I'm writing a song:

'I'm the best in the forest.

I'm the fastest swimmer of all …'

Bear: That is a silly song!
Bears are fast. Turtles are slow.

Turtle 1: Not when we are swimming.

I can swim faster than you can run.

Bear: That is ridiculous. Let's have a race.

Turtle 1: OK! Let's meet at the pond tomorrow.

I can swim, you can run.

Narrator: The animals come to watch the race.

Rabbit & Frog: We're cheering for Turtle.

Deer & Fox: We're cheering for Bear.

Crow: Ready, steady, go!

Turtle 1: Hurry up, Bear! I'm going faster than you.

Bear:	Wow! That turtle is swimming fast!
Turtle 2:	Hurry up, Bear!
Bear:	I'm running as fast as I can.
Turtle 3:	Look at me, Bear. I'm winning!
Bear:	Oh no, I'm losing the race.
Crow:	Turtle is the winner!
Deer & Fox:	Turtle's won the race!
Rabbit & Frog:	Hooray for Turtle!
Bear:	I'm going to my cave. I don't want to see anyone.
Deer:	I'm sorry, Bear. Don't feel sad.
Fox:	It's just a silly race, Bear.
Narrator:	When everyone is gone, Turtle taps on the ice three times.
Turtle 4:	You can come out now.
Turtles 1, 2 & 3:	We did it! We won!
Turtle 4:	Yes, turtles are not fast, but we are clever!

2 Talk about the story.

Why do the turtles want to teach Bear a lesson?

How many turtles were really in the race?

Do you think the race was fair or unfair?

3 Values: Understanding feelings

How does Bear feel at the end of the race?

excited   angry   upset   happy   sad   confused   tired

What do Deer and Fox say to make Bear feel better?

4 Write a conversation.

Imagine that a friend has lost a race and is feeling sad and upset.

What can you say to help your friend feel better?

Write a short conversation. Look at the box for some ideas.

Read the conversation with your partner.

> **Friend:** I hate losing races. I'm going home. I don't want to see anyone.
> **You:** _____
> **Friend:** _____

I'm sorry you're sad.
Thank you.

Do you want to play something else?
Yes! Let's …

It's just a silly race.
I know.

5 Act out the play.

> 3.7 Project challenge

Work on the project with a partner or group. Then share with the class.

A: Lead an action game

Write ten body words on cards.
(Look at the Picture dictionary on page 167 for ideas.)

Play a game with your class.

Pick two cards. Say the words
as you ask the question:

**Can you put your elbow
on your ear?**

Your classmates will try!
They will say,

Yes, we can!
or
No, we can't!

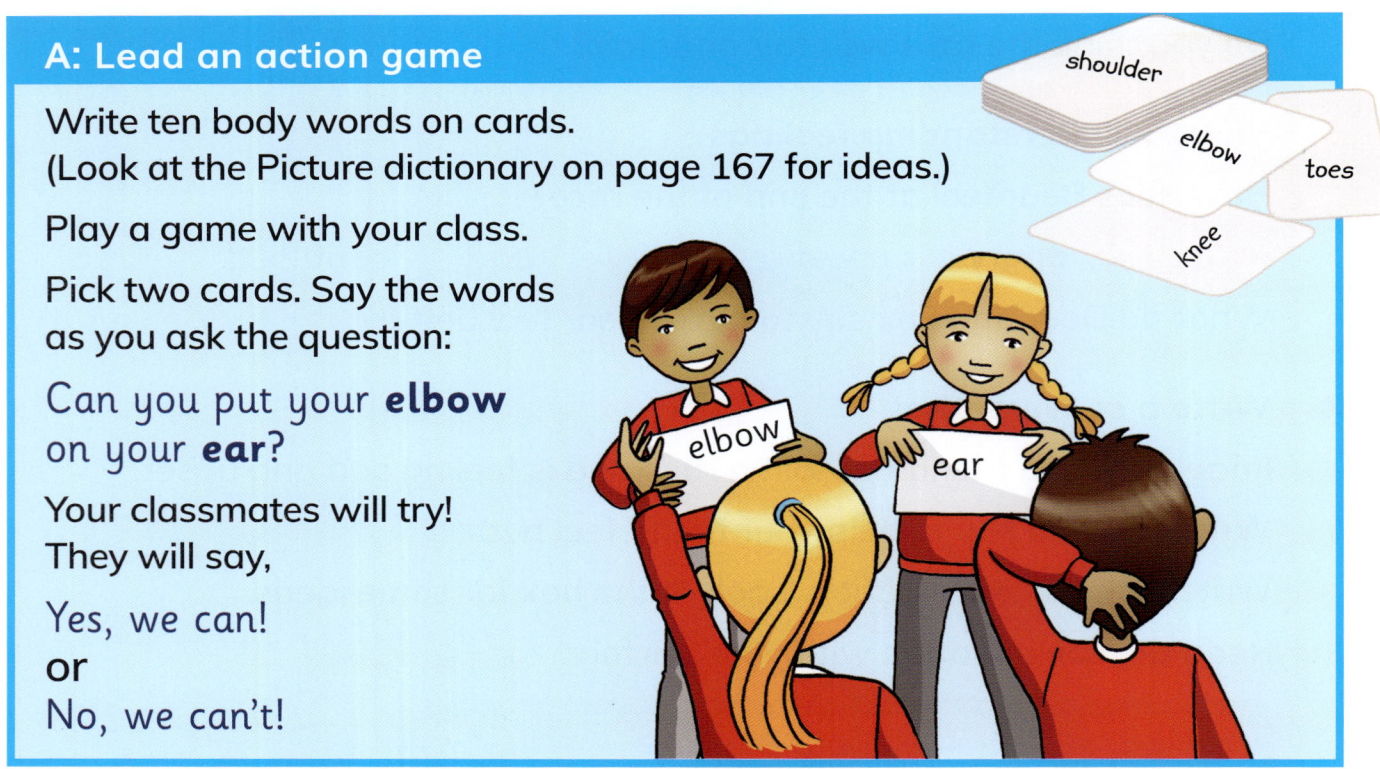

shoulder
elbow
toes
knee

B: Write an animal riddle: Who am I?

Read this riddle. Can you guess the answer?

Write your own animal riddles.
Cover the answer with a piece of paper.

Read the riddles to your class.
Can they guess the answers?

I am _____ and _____.
I like _____ and _____.
You can find me _____ or _____.

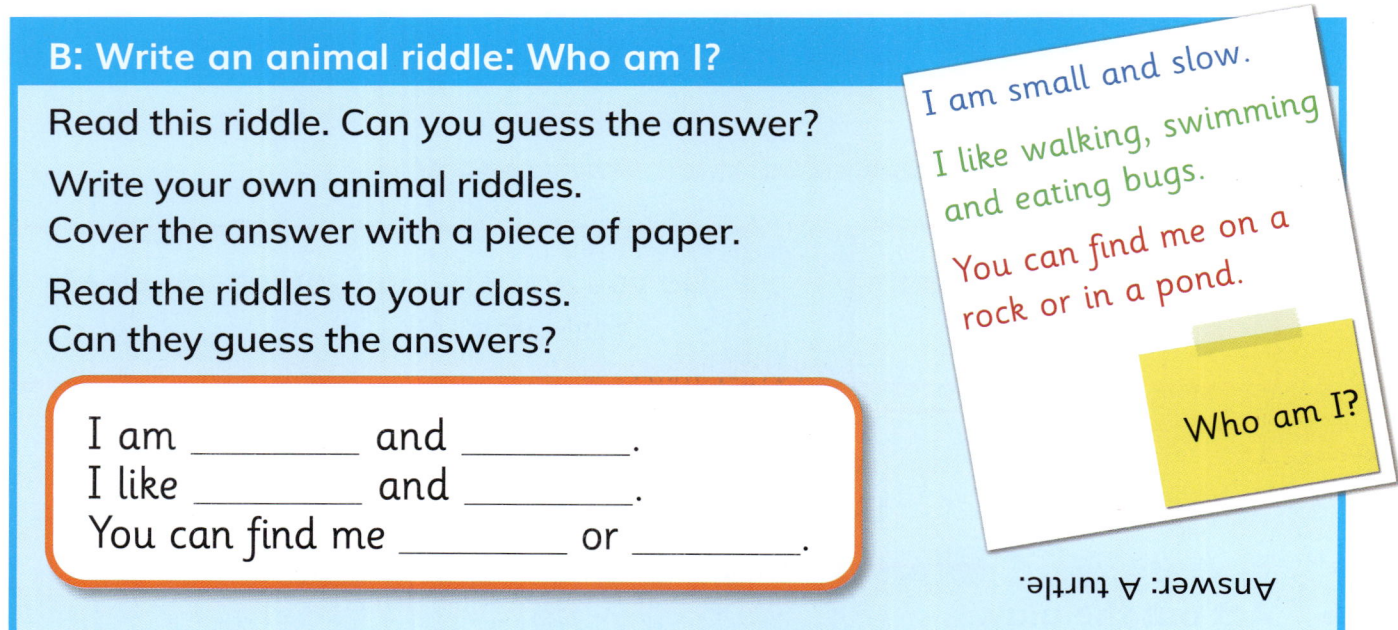

I am small and slow.

I like walking, swimming and eating bugs.

You can find me on a rock or in a pond.

Who am I?

Answer: A turtle.

C: Make a counting book: Frog maths

Make a maths book about frogs, with 10 pages.

The first page has 1 frog. The second page has 2 frogs.

The last page has 10 frogs.

1 frog
2 eyes
4 legs

2 frogs
4 eyes
___ legs

How many legs do 2 frogs have?

Make a cover for your book. Write the title and authors on the cover.

Think of the three projects you have done
(for Unit 1, Unit 2 and Unit 3).
Which project do you think was the best? Why?

Look what I can do!

- I can talk about ways I can move.
- I can read and talk about birds and what they can do.
- I can talk about what people are doing.
- I can read and write words with long vowel sounds.
- I can read, talk about and act out a play.

› Check your progress 1
Treasure hunt

START

You need:

- 2 to 3 players
- a different game marker for each player
- number cards.

Directions

- Take a number card.
- Count and move your game marker on the game track.
- Read and answer the questions.
- Read and follow the directions.

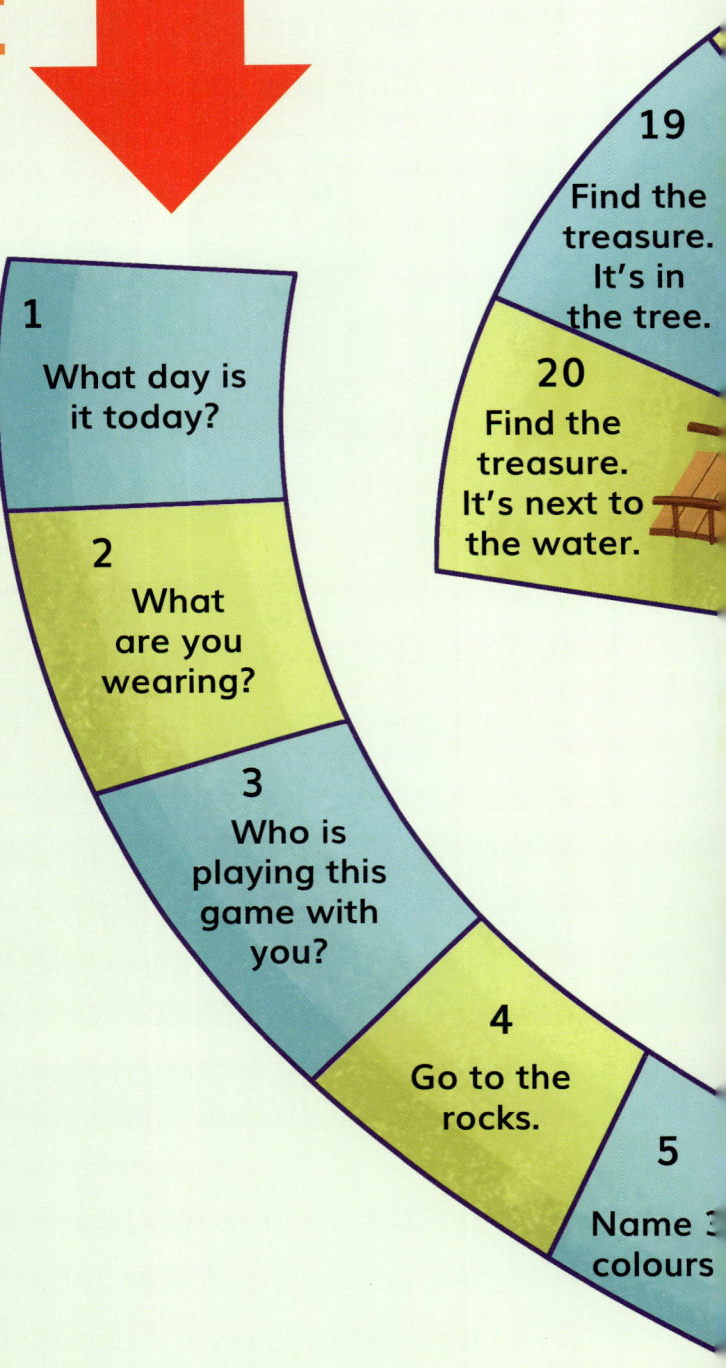

1 What day is it today?

2 What are you wearing?

3 Who is playing this game with you?

4 Go to the rocks.

5 Name 3 colours

19 Find the treasure. It's in the tree.

20 Find the treasure. It's next to the water.

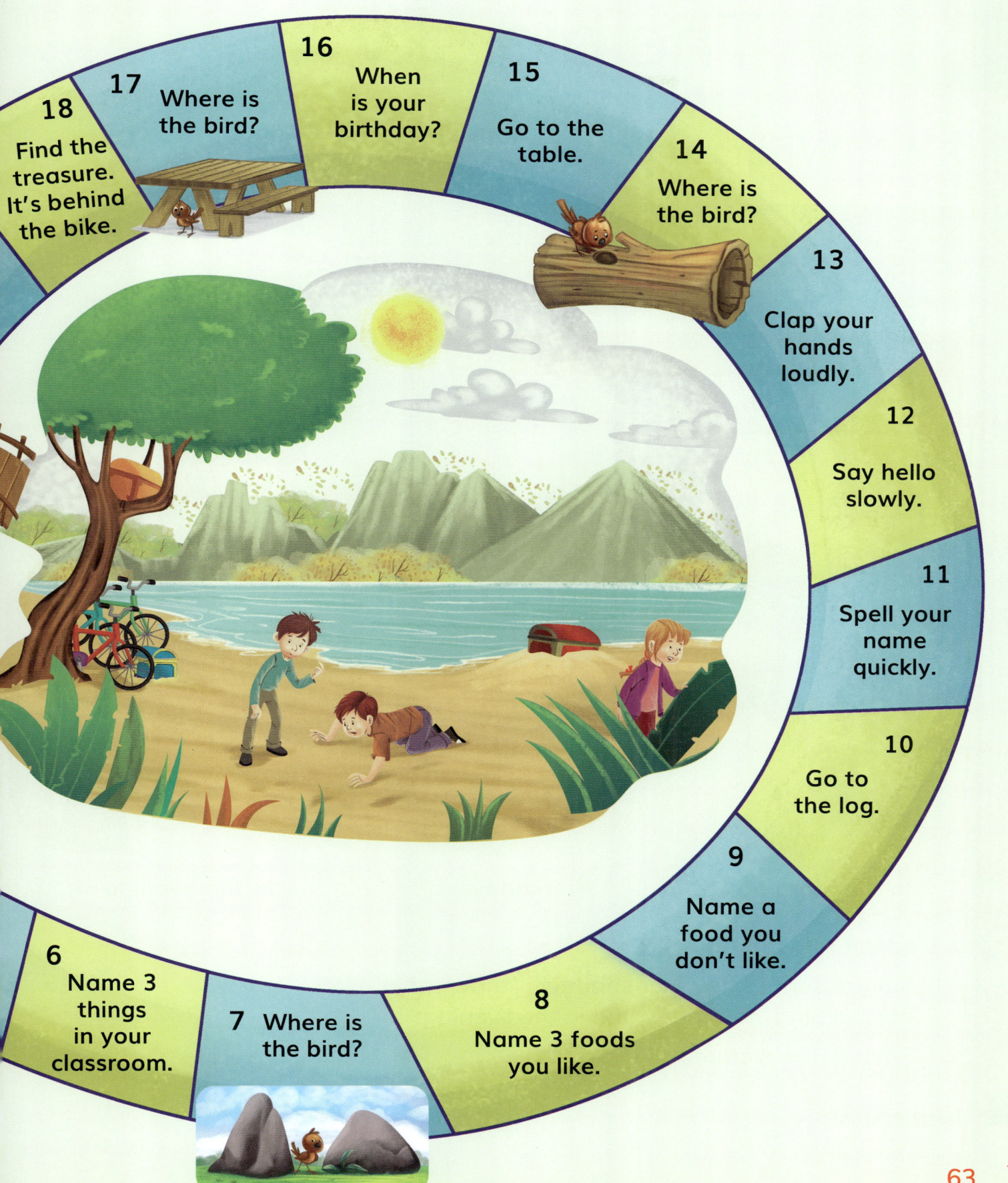

18 Find the treasure. It's behind the bike.

17 Where is the bird?

16 When is your birthday?

15 Go to the table.

14 Where is the bird?

13 Clap your hands loudly.

12 Say hello slowly.

11 Spell your name quickly.

10 Go to the log.

9 Name a food you don't like.

8 Name 3 foods you like.

7 Where is the bird?

6 Name 3 things in your classroom.

4 ▸ The big sky

⟩ 4.1 What do you know about shadows?

We are going to...

- talk about shadows.

Getting started

What are shadows?

In the morning

At midday

In the evening

 1 Listen and point.

Sally describes how her shadow is different in the morning, at midday and in the evening.

Point to the pictures as she talks.

 Watch this!

2 **Listen, point and say.**

sky   low   high   shadow   long   short

3 **Look again at the pictures of Sally.**

a   In the morning, is the Sun high or low in the sky?

b   In the morning, is Sally's shadow long or short?

c   At midday, is the Sun high or low in the sky?

d   At midday, is Sally's shadow long or short?

4 **Look out of the window.**

a   What colour is the sky today?

b   Do you see shadows outside?

c   What shadows do you see?

d   To make a shadow, you need light. What makes light outside?

 5 **Read, listen and act out the poem.**

My shadow

I have a little shadow that goes in and out with me,

And what can be the use of him is more than I can see.

He is very, very like me from the heels up to the head;

And I see him jump before me, when I jump into my bed.

Robert Louis Stevenson

> 4.2 Light and shadow

We are going to...

- talk about and do experiments with shadows.

1 **Read the description.**

What is making the shadow? Find the matching shadow on a sticker.

people riding bikes

two hands

a helicopter

an insect

2 **Telling time with a shadow**

A sundial is like a clock. A clock uses hands to point at the numbers. A sundial uses a shadow. Look at the sundials. What time is it?

  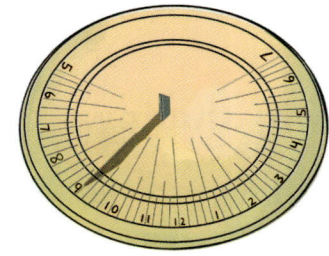

3 **Make a sundial.**

Step 1: Put a ball of clay on a paper plate.
Step 2: Push a pencil into the clay.
Step 3: Leave your sundial in a sunny place.
Step 4: Mark the shadow in the morning and in the afternoon.
Step 5: Look how the shadow moves.

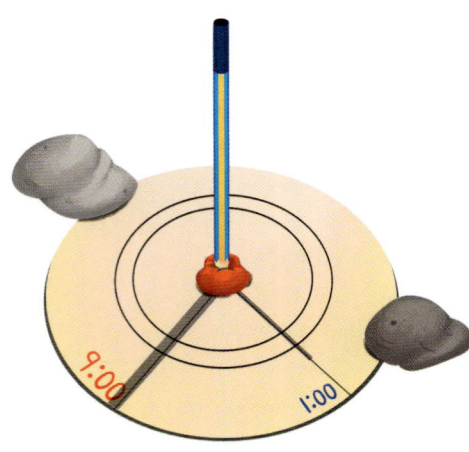

4 Experiment with shadows.

Outside, the Sun is the source of light that makes shadows. Inside the classroom, a torch can be the source of light.

You will need a small toy or object. Pretend your torch is the Sun.

Move the torch in a half circle over the toy, moving from morning to midday to evening. How does the shadow change?

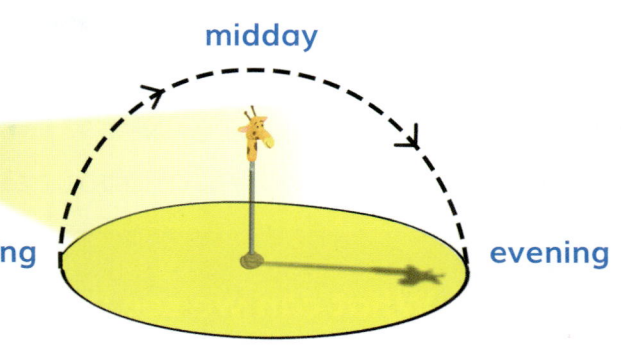

5 Try this!

Place a strip of tape a distance away from the toy. Turn on your torch.

Can you make the shadow of the toy touch the tape?

Do you need to hold your torch high or low?
(Hint: Does the shadow need to be long or short?)

Now place the piece of tape close to the toy. Try to make the shadow of the toy touch the tape.

Do you need to hold your torch high or low?
(Hint: Does the shadow need to be long or short?)

6 Count the shadows.

If you shine 2 torches at an object, how many shadows will you see?

Make a prediction (a guess), then try it! Was your prediction correct?

> 4.3 The Sun, Earth, Moon and stars

Earth

Sun

Moon

We are going to...

- read and write about the Sun, Earth, Moon and stars.

 47 **1 What can we see in the sky?**

The Sun

The Sun is a star that is at the centre of our solar system. Earth and seven other **planets** circle around the Sun. Earth is the third planet away from the Sun.

The Sun is the only star that we can see in the day. The Sun gives us heat and light. Without the Sun, there would be no life on Earth.

The stars

Nobody can count all the stars in the sky. There are too many.

Our sun is the closest star to Earth. All the other stars are much farther away.

Some of the stars are bigger than our Sun and some of the stars are smaller.

Because they are so far away, all the stars look very tiny.

Key word

planet: 8 planets circle around our Sun

The Moon

The Moon circles around Earth.

We can see the Moon because the Sun shines light on it.

Sometimes we see a whole round Moon. Sometimes we see only part of the Moon.

When people look at a full Moon, sometimes they see a picture. In some places, people say they see a man in the Moon. In other places, people see a Moon rabbit or a Moon frog.

Why do we have day and night?

The Sun shines on our planet, Earth.

Earth turns slowly round and round.

Part of the Earth faces the Sun.

Part of the Earth faces away from the Sun.

When it is light, we have day.

When it is dark, we have night.

Sun

Sunlight

Earth

2 Try it out

You need:

- A torch (Sun)
- A globe or ball (Earth).

1 Put a sticker on Earth where you live.

2 Shine the torch on the globe or ball.

3 Turn the globe or ball slowly.

4 When the sticker faces the Sun, it is day.

5 When the sticker does not face the Sun, it is night.

When it is daytime where you live, it is night somewhere else on Earth.

Look on a globe. Name a place on the other side of the globe where it is now night.

3 Write about it.

With your partner, say an interesting fact about:

the Sun **Earth** **the Moon** **stars**

Draw a picture and write one sentence for each.

> 4.4 Using the past simple

We are going to...

- talk and write about what people did in the past.

1   Read the poem.

Then do the actions.

A trip to outer space

We travelled by spaceship to outer space,
Far, far away. We were very brave.
We waved at the Earth.
We watched the Earth get smaller and smaller.

We travelled by spaceship to outer space,
Far, far away. We were very excited.
We jumped out of the spaceship.
We walked on planet Mars.

We travelled by spaceship to outer space,
Far, far away. We were very tired.
We climbed back into the spaceship.
We travelled home to planet Earth.

Language detective

Verbs ending in -ed

Look at the words in red that end in **-ed**.

Those words are verbs. They tell us what the children did.

Find other verbs in the poem that end in **-ed**.

2 **What did you do yesterday?**

Interview your partner. Your partner can choose verbs from the box.

Then write what your partner did yesterday.

> What did you do yesterday?

> I **walked to** the park and I **played with** my sister.

played with (Who?)

talked to (Who?)

walked to (Where?)

watched (What?)

Yesterday, Peng walked to the park and he played with his sister.

 49 **3** **Listen and point to the picture.**

Then answer the questions.

Now	In the past
I am	I was
She is	She was
They are	They were

a   Where is Paco now? Where was he this afternoon?

b   Where are Paco's sisters now? Where were they this afternoon?

c   Where was Paco's mum this afternoon?

d   Where are you now? Where were you last night?

> 4.5 Long i

We are going to...

- read and write words with long **i** spellings.

 1 **Words with the long i sound**

Listen and repeat. Do you hear the long **i** sound in each word?

Find the words that end in these spellings: **-ite**, **-ine**, **-ight**.

line   night   shine   kite   right

Which words rhyme with **bite**?

2 **Clap and say.**

Clap the syllables and say these words. What sound does the final **-y** make in a one-syllable word? In a two-syllable word?

fly   rainy   cloudy   cry   dry   sunny

 3 **Listen to the spelling and write the word.**

Point to the picture and say the word.

4 **Sticker activity**  sky   night   sunshine

Read the words. Listen for the long **i** sound. Find the stickers.
Put the stickers on the Nature page (page 175) of the Picture dictionary.

5 **Find and say.**

A compound word is a big word made of two little words.

Find the little words in each big word.

sunshine = **sun** + **shine**

Say each word. Find the matching definition and picture.

sunrise	when the sun rises in the morning	a	
sunglasses	a boat with a sail	b	
raincoat	a coat to wear in the rain	c	
sailboat	dark glasses to wear in the sunlight	d	

 52

6 **Listen and sing.**

The words to this song are a type of weather forecast.

If the sky is red at night, be happy! There will be good weather tomorrow.

If the sky is red in the morning, take warning! Get your raincoat. There will be bad weather later in the day.

Which words in the song rhyme?

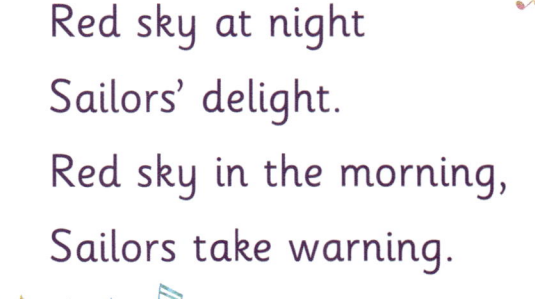

Red sky at night
Sailors' delight.
Red sky in the morning,
Sailors take warning.

> 4.6 Our trip to the Moon

We are going to...

- read and talk about a make-believe trip to the Moon.

1   Before you read

What do you know about the Moon?
What questions do you have about the Moon?
Make two lists.

Our trip to the Moon

Last week, we went on a field trip.
Professor Clark took us to the Moon!

It took two days to travel to the Moon.
It was fun to float around in the spaceship!

When we wanted to nap, we strapped
ourselves into sleeping bags.

When we arrived at the Moon, Professor
Clark gave us our spacesuits.

Why do we need spacesuits on the Moon?

- The Moon is very hot during the day. The spacesuit keeps us cool.
- There is no air on the Moon. The backpack on the spacesuit gives us air to breathe.

74

On the Moon there is less gravity than on Earth.

That means we weighed much less on the Moon.

We jumped over craters. We could jump very high.

We looked at the Earth shining big and bright in the sky.

Why does Earth look so bright?

- The Earth looks big and bright in the black sky of the Moon. It is bright because it is lit by the light of the Sun.
- Earth is 4 times as big as the Moon, so it looks bigger and brighter than the Moon.

75

Professor Clark said we could take one Moon rock home with us.

The soil on the Moon was dry and dusty.

Back at school, we looked for answers to our questions.

We wrote reports and drew pictures.

We learned a lot of things about the Moon!

2 List the facts about the Moon.

This story is about a make-believe field trip to the Moon, but it also has a lot of true facts about the Moon.

With your class, look through the story.
Make a list of the facts you have learned about the Moon.

3 Find the compound words.

What compound words can you find in this story?

4 Values: Wondering and learning about the world around us

Good scientists wonder about the world around them.

They look carefully, ask questions, and search for the answers.

Good students do the same thing!

Look at the list of questions you made before you read this story.

Do you know the answer to any of those questions now?

5 Writing questions, finding answers

Work with a partner or a small group.

Write three new questions about the Moon or about travelling to the Moon.

Choose one question. Look in a book or on the computer to find the answer.

Write a short report. Look at the 3 reports in the story for ideas.

> **Writing tip**
>
> A sentence that is a question ends with a question mark.
>
> How big is the Moon?

› 4.7 Project challenge

Work on the project with a partner or group. Then share with the class.

A: Make a game: What did you do yesterday?

1 Write the **past tense** of these verbs on 8 cards:

   play talk learn use touch walk watch listen

2 Write these words on 4 time cards:

   yesterday   last night   last week   last year

3 Play the game with your class. Your team will pick a time card and a verb card.

   Ask a question and say the verb. Your classmates will make up answers, using those words.

What did you do **last night**?

Played.

Last night I **played** with my brother.

B: Write a book about the Sun

1 First, brainstorm ideas together. What facts will you write?

2 Look up information about the Sun on the Internet or in books.

3 Write 1 or 2 sentences about the Sun. Use the Writer's Checklist to check your writing.

4 Use a plate to trace a circle on a piece of paper. Cut out the circle and write your sentences about the Sun on it. Draw a picture.

5 Staple the pages together with a cover on top. Write a title and the names of the authors on the cover.

The Sun helps plants grow.

C: Make a weather chart

1 Make weather cards with pictures and words.

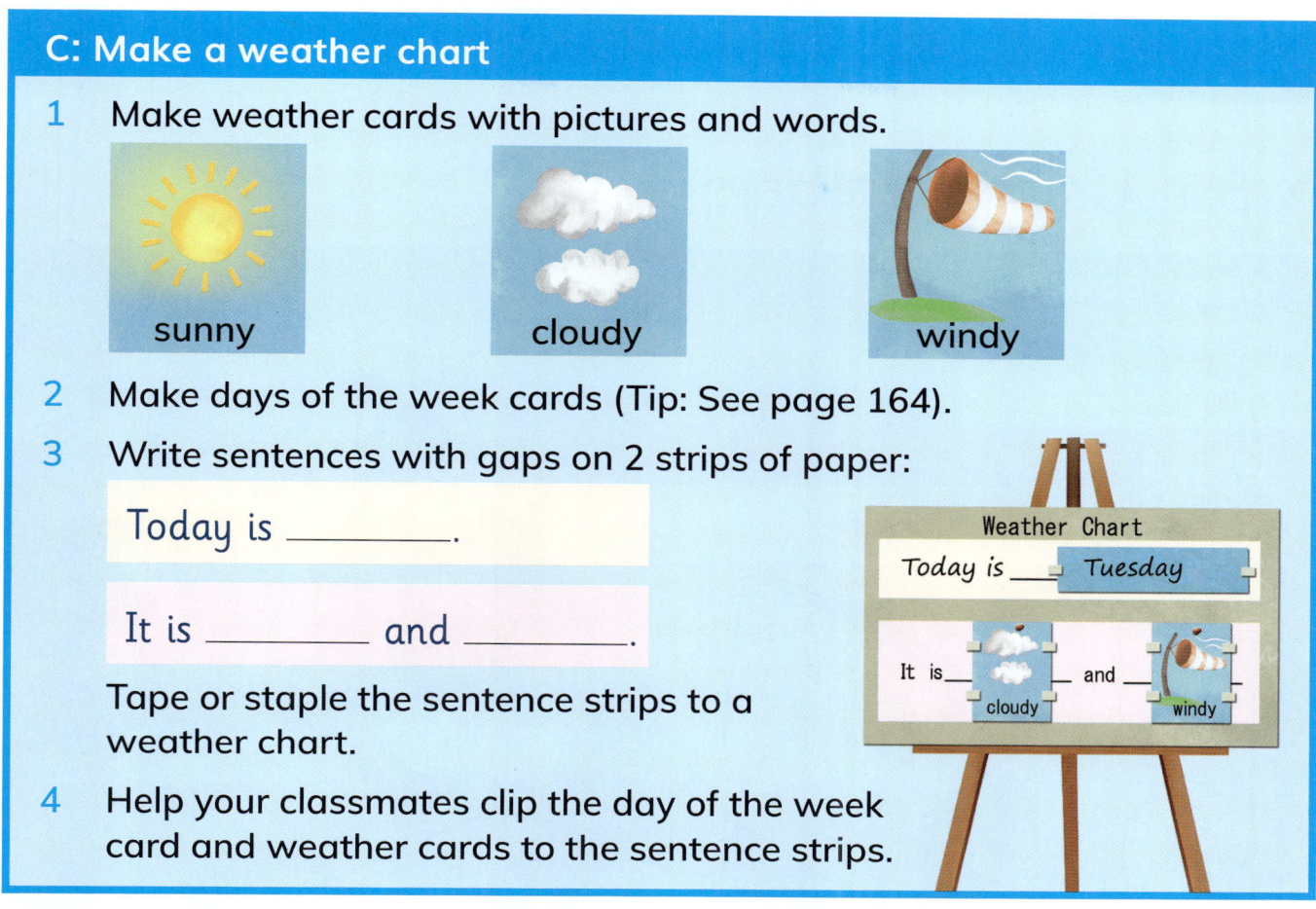

sunny   cloudy   windy

2 Make days of the week cards (Tip: See page 164).

3 Write sentences with gaps on 2 strips of paper:

Today is _____.

It is _____ and _____.

Tape or staple the sentence strips to a weather chart.

4 Help your classmates clip the day of the week card and weather cards to the sentence strips.

How many people worked together on your project?
What is your favourite number of people to work with?
Why do you think that's a good number for doing a project?

Look what I can do!

- I can talk about shadows.
- I can do experiments with shadows.
- I can read and write about the Sun, Earth, Moon and stars.
- I can talk and write about what people did in the past.
- I can read and write words with long i spellings.
- I can read and talk about a make-believe trip to the Moon.

5 ▶ Let's measure

▸ 5.1 Using numbers

We are going to...

- count to 100.

Getting started

When do we use numbers?

Jack   60 cm

Maria   48 cm

Liz   72 cm

🎧 54   **1   Listen for the numbers.**

The children in this class are using numbers to count, measure and tell time.

Point to the children you hear.
Listen, then answer these questions:

a   How many big circles are there?

b   How far did Carlos jump?

c   What time is it?

🎥 Watch this!

2 **Listen, point and say.**

Count in tens.

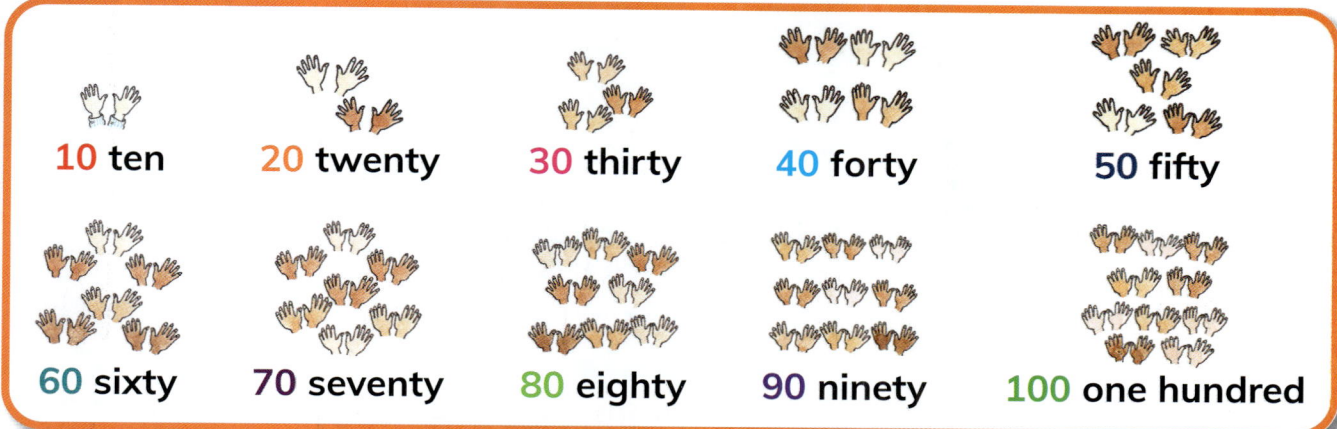

10 ten   **20 twenty**   **30 thirty**   **40 forty**   **50 fifty**

60 sixty   **70 seventy**   **80 eighty**   **90 ninety**   **100 one hundred**

3 **Count the shapes.**

Look at the chart of shapes in the big picture.
There are 10 shapes in each row.

How many shapes are there altogether?

Point to the rows and count in tens.

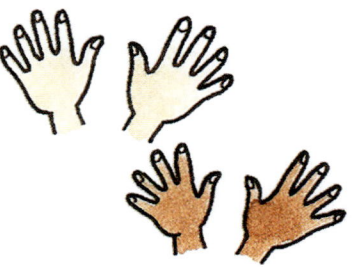

 **4** **Listen, read and sing.**

There are ten children singing this song in the big picture.
Do you see them?

How many children have their fingers in the air?

How many fingers are in the air altogether?
(Hint: Point and count in tens!)

10 little, 20 little, 30 little fingers.

40 little, 50 little, 60 little fingers.

70 little, 80 little, 90 little fingers.

100 little fingers in the air!

100 little, 90 little, 80 little fingers …

> 5.2 Shapes, patterns and numbers

We are going to...

- **name and describe shapes.**

1 Name the shapes. Listen, point and repeat.

circle   square   triangle   rectangle   heart

2 **Explore the pattern.**

a Look at the **first row**.
What do you notice about all of the shapes?
What shapes do you see in the **second, third, fourth** and **fifth** rows?

b Look at the **first column**.
Are the shapes big or little? What colour are they?

c What do you notice about the size and colour of the shapes in the other columns?

1	2	3	4	5	6	7	8	9	10
11	12	13	14	15	16	17	18	19	20
21	22	23	24	25	26	27	28	29	30
31	32	33	34	35	36	37	38	39	40
41	42	43	44	45	46	47	48	49	50

3 **Place the stickers in the correct position in the chart.**

Complete the pattern!

4 **Describe the shapes.**

Look at the chart. Find the matching description.

a What is shape number 3?

b What is shape number 19?

c What is shape number 21?

d What is shape number 37?

e What is shape number 45?

A big red triangle

A little purple circle

A little orange heart

A little yellow square

A big green rectangle

> **Language detective**
>
> Which do we say first in English: the **colour** word or the **size** word?
>
> **big** red shapes   little yellow shapes

5 **How far can you jump?**

Look at the big picture in lesson 5.1 (page 80). Find Carlos, the boy who is jumping.

His friend Luis measured how far Carlos jumped. How many centimetres did he jump?

How far can you and your classmates jump? Try it!

Write how many centimetres on a piece of paper.

Then put the papers in order, from smallest to biggest.

> 5.3 How did people measure long ago?

We are going to...

- measure and say how long something is.

1 Measuring in Ancient Egypt

Long ago in Egypt, people **measured** with their fingers, hands and arms.

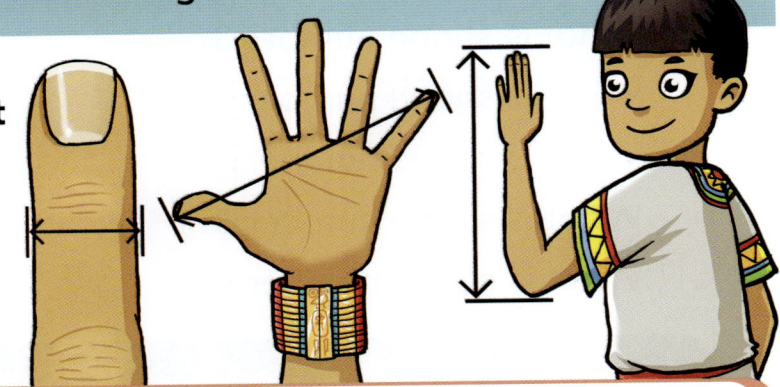

Try it out!

How many **fingers** long is this line?
How many **hands** tall is this line?
How many **arms** long is your table?

Key word

measure: find the exact size or amount

2 Measuring in Ancient Rome

Long ago in Rome, people measured in **footsteps**.

Try it out!
Measure your classroom in footsteps.
How many footsteps long is it?
Ask your teacher to measure your classroom in footsteps.
Is your teacher's answer the same as your answer? Why not?

3 Measuring today

Today we use the metric system to measure.
We use centimetres and metres.
There are 100 centimetres in a metre.
This line is 1 centimetre long. ___

4 Centimetres or metres?

We use **centimetres** to measure small things.
We use **metres** to measure big things.
What would you use to measure these things?

	Your school hall	**centimetres**	**metres**
	A leaf	**centimetres**	**metres**
	A fence	**centimetres**	**metres**

5 How long is it?

Use a ruler to measure these pictures.

How long is it?

It's 3 centimetres long.

a   a paper clip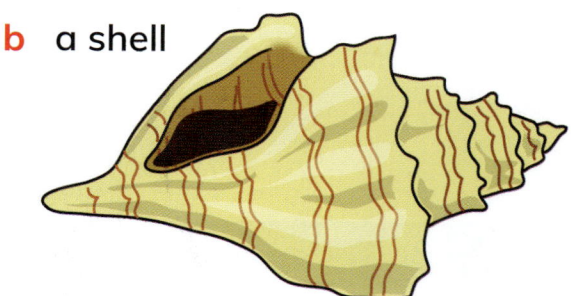

b   a shell

c   a fish

d   a paintbrush

> 5.4 Using the past simple (irregular verbs)

We are going to...

- **talk and write about what people did in the past.**

58 **1   Listen, point and repeat.**

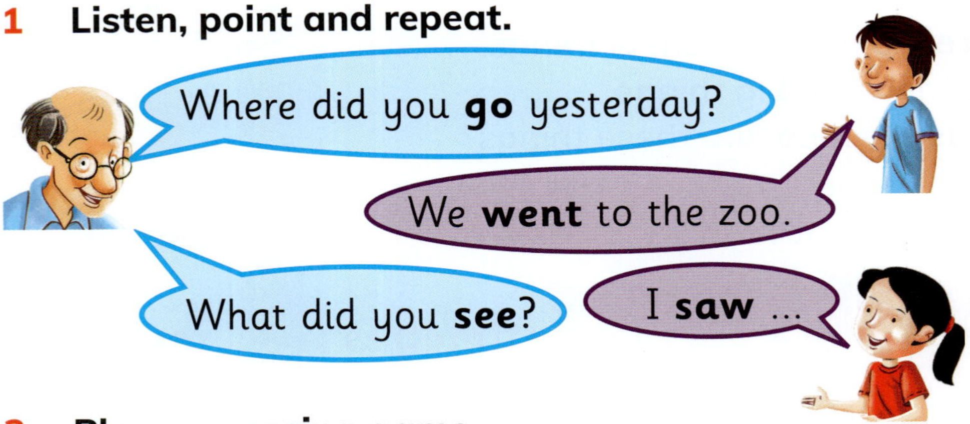

Where did you **go** yesterday?

We **went** to the zoo.

What did you **see**?

I **saw** ...

a lion

an elephant

a giraffe

a cheetah

2   Play a guessing game.

What did you see at the zoo?

Draw a picture and write a sentence: I saw _____.

Your classmates will try to guess the animal.

Did you see an antelope?

No, I didn't.

Yes, I did!

Did you see a lion?

a chimpanzee

an antelope

Language detective

Some verbs add -ed to make the past but other verbs are different!

see → saw   He **saw** a bear.   eat → ate   He **ate** an apple.

As you read the next story, look for the past simple of these verbs:

look   think   draw   laugh   make   say

3 Read a maths story from India.

Birbal was a wise man who lived in India many years ago.

What did King Akbar ask Birbal to do?

How did Birbal solve the problem?

Clever Birbal

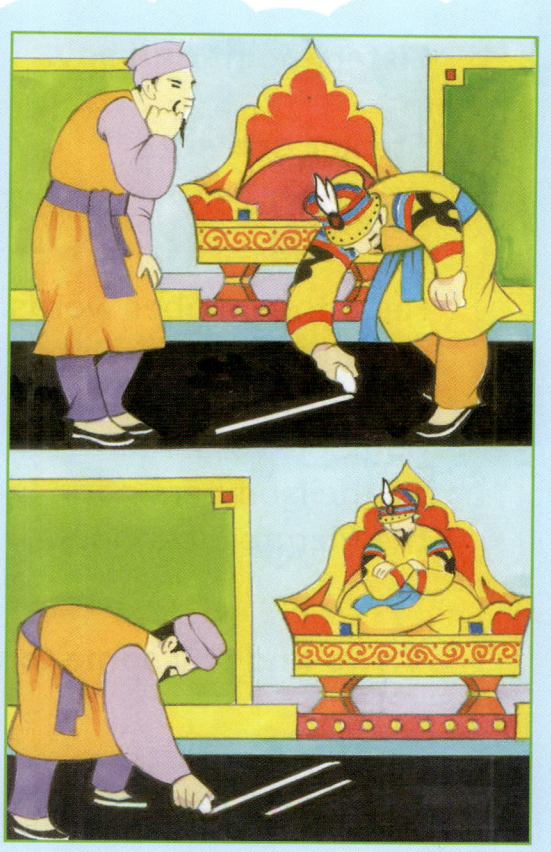

One day, King Akbar picked up a piece of chalk and drew a line on the floor. 'Birbal,' he said to his friend, 'I want you to make this line shorter. But you cannot rub out the ends of the line.'

Birbal looked at the line and thought. Then he drew a long line under King Akbar's line. 'Look,' said Birbal. 'My line is longer than your line. So your line is shorter!'

King Akbar laughed. 'You are right, Birbal,' he said. 'You made my line shorter. What a clever answer!'

Act out the story with a partner. As you act, draw the lines on some paper.

4 Turn to the Actions page (page 174) in your Picture dictionary.

Say the present simple and past simple of each verb.

Then, think of an action verb that is <u>not</u> on the Picture dictionary page.

Draw a picture and write the present simple and past simple words in the box at the bottom corner.

〉 5.5 Words that sound the same

We are going to...

- **read and write words that sound the same.**

 1 **Listen, point and say.**

2 **Sticker activity**

| one | two | four | eight |

Read the number words. Look at the pictures and speech bubbles. Find a word that sounds the same as each number word. Put the number stickers on the Numbers page (page 166) of the Picture dictionary.

I won two prizes.

I won one prize.

I won two prizes too!

I ate eight bananas. These four are for you.

3 **Write and say some tongue-twisters using these words.**

eight – ate   **four** – **for**

Ed <u>ate</u> <u>eight</u> eggs.   _____ flags _____ Fran.

 4 **Read and sing!**

Find the words that sound the same.

One-one was a racehorse.
Two-two was one, too.
One-one won one race.
Two-two won one, too.

5   **Describing animals: *clever*, *fast*, *heavy***

Read about each animal. Find the matching picture.
Choose a word to describe the animal.

Then think of another animal that is also **clever**, **fast** or **heavy**.
Write the sentences.

a   An African elephant weighs the
    same as 100 men.

    An elephant is _____!

    A _____ is _____ too.

b   A parrot can learn to talk. It can count,
    name colours and do maths.

    A parrot is _____!

    A _____ is _____ too.

c   A very good runner can run 12 metres in a second.

    A cheetah can run 30 metres in a second.

    A cheetah is _____!

    A _____ is _____ too.

 6   **Count in twos.**

Use the number line to count in twos to 12.
Then join in with the poem.

Make up a new verse of the poem starting with '**22, 24 ...**'

2, 4, 6, 8. Mary's at the cottage gate.

Eating cherries on a plate – 2, 4, 6, 8.

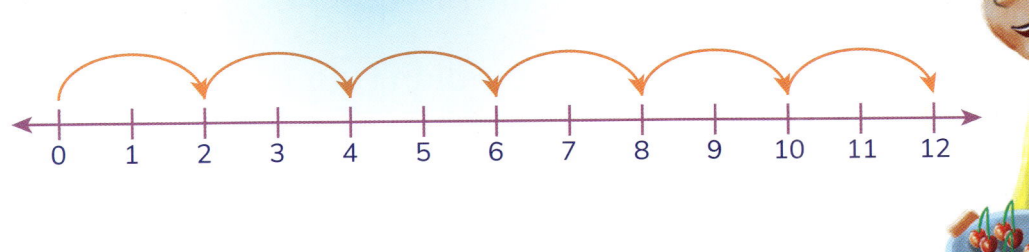

89   〉

> 5.6 Many ways to count to ten

We are going to...

- **read, discuss and act out a story.**

Reading tip

This story is a folktale from Africa.

1   Read and listen.

Read and listen as far as the bottom of page 91.
Then stop and make a prediction. What do you think will happen next?
(Hint: Look at the pictures.)

Many ways to count to ten

A long time ago, Leopard was the king of the forest. One day, he said, 'I'm getting old and tired. It's time to choose a new king.' He put up signs in the forest.

All the animals came to the contest. King Leopard said, 'Thank you for coming. Let me explain the contest. You must throw this spear high into the air and quickly count to ten. You must say "ten" before the spear hits the ground. The winner of the contest will be the new king of the forest.'

The elephant was the first to try.

'I'm very big,' he said. 'I think I can do it.' The elephant threw the spear high into the air. '1, 2, 3, 4, 5, ...,' he counted loudly. Boom! The spear hit the ground.

'I'm sorry, Elephant,' said the king. 'You didn't do it. You didn't count to ten.'

The water ox was second.

'I'm very strong,' he said.
'I think I can do it.'
The water ox threw the
spear high into the air, '1,
2, 3, 4, 5, 6,' he counted
loudly. Boom! The spear
hit the ground.

'I'm sorry, Water Ox,' said
the king. 'You didn't do it.
You didn't count to ten.'

The chimpanzee was third.

'I can count very quickly,' he said. 'I think I can do it.'
The chimpanzee threw the spear high into the air,
'1, 2, 3, 4, 5, 6, 7, 8,' he
counted quickly. Boom!
The spear hit the ground.

'I'm sorry, Chimpanzee,'
said the king. 'You didn't
do it. You didn't count
to ten.'

The little antelope was next.

'Hello, King Leopard,' he said, quietly. 'Can I try?'

'Of course, little friend,' said the king. 'Here is the spear.'

The tiny antelope jumped high into the air as he threw the spear. '2, 4, 6, 8, 10!' counted the antelope. Boom!
The spear hit the ground.

'You did it!' said the king. 'Well done, Little Antelope! You counted to ten in twos. What a clever idea! The forest has a new and very clever king!'

'Three cheers for King Antelope,' cried the animals. 'Hip, hip, hurray! Hip, hip, hurray! Hip, hip, hurray!'

2   **Talk about it.**

a   Why did King Leopard want to choose a new king?

b   What were the rules of the contest?

c   Which animals took part in the contest?

d   Which animals counted loudly?

e   Which animal counted quickly?

f   Which of these words describe Little Antelope?

| big | strong | tiny | clever | loud | quiet |

g   What was Little Antelope's clever idea?

h   Do you think Little Antelope will be a good king?
Why or why not?

3   **Act out the story.**

Listen to the story again. Use puppets to act out the story.

4   **Values: Good qualities we admire**

There are lots of good qualities a person can have.

Discuss and act out these words.

kind   friendly   happy   funny   clever   quick

strong   fair   honest   brave   patient

•   Choose the 2 qualities that you like
best about yourself, in a friend and
in a teacher.

5   **Writing: Describe and explain**

Describe the qualities that you like most
in your friends.

I like friends who are
_____ and _____.

They make me feel
_____.

〉 5.7 Project challenge

Work on the project with a partner or group. Then share with the class.

A: Make a picture with 100 shapes

You will need coloured paper, scissors and glue.

Cut out 10 sets of shapes. For example:

10 **red** squares	10 **yellow** triangles
10 **blue** squares	10 **red** rectangles
10 **yellow** squares	10 **blue** rectangles
10 **red** triangles	10 **red** hearts
10 **blue** triangles	10 **blue** hearts

Use the shapes to make a picture.

Write three questions about your picture, for example:

* How many triangles are in our picture?
* How many **blue** shapes are in our picture?
* How many **red** hearts are in our picture?

B: Have a contest

Choose a contest to do in **one minute**:

* How far can you count in English?
* How many times can you hop?
* How many times can you write your name?

Time each person.

C: Make a measuring book

Think of 6 questions. For example:

- How long is a new pencil?
- How long is Huang's hand?
- How tall is the teacher's chair?

Write each question on a page.

Measure the object. Write the answer.

Make a flap to cover the answer.

Your classmates must try to guess the answer.

How long is my hand?

11 cm

What part of your project was the hardest?

Look what I can do!

I can count to 100.	○	○
I can name and describe shapes.	○	○
I can measure and say how long something is.	○	○
I can talk and write about what people did in the past.	○	○
I can read and write words that sound the same, like *one / won* and *two / too*.	○	○
I can read, discuss and act out a story.	○	○

6 > All about bugs

> 6.1 Bugs and other garden animals

We are going to...

- read and talk about insects.

Getting started

What do you know about bugs?

Look at the picture for more ideas.

1 **Listen and point to the animals.**

Which animals are <u>not</u> talked about?

Which of these animals live near your home?

Watch this!

2 **Listen, point and say.**

Then answer the questions.

web

butterfly   bee   cricket   ant   worm   spider

3 **Where are they?**

Look at the picture and say the sentences.
Use the words in the box.

above	between
in front of	on

a   The ___ is _____ a rock.

b   The ___ is _____ the cricket.

c   The ___ is _____ two branches.

d   The ___ is _____ the web.

e   The ___ are flying _____ the flowers.

 4 **Read, listen and act out the poem.**

One, two, three!

There's a bug on me.

Where did it go?

I don't know.

5 **Write some animal clues.**

Look at the big picture.

Choose an animal. Write a description.

Can your partner find the animal?

It has two legs.
It eats worms.

It's an insect.
It has four
blue wings.

> 6.2 Crickets and other insects

We are going to...

- **learn about insects.**

A cricket is an insect.

antennae

wings

6 legs

 1 **What is an insect?**

Listen and look at the diagram.
Then answer the questions.

a   How many legs does an insect have?

b   Do all insects have antennae?

c   Do all insects have wings?

2 **Sticker activity**

| ant | bee | butterfly | worm | cricket | spider |

Look at the animals on the stickers. Are they insects or not?
Count the legs. Put the stickers on the chart.

Then, add one more animal to the 'not insects' column.

Draw a picture. Write its name.

insects	not insects

3 **Listen to this interview with Maylin and her grandpa.**

Find out the answers to these questions.

a What does Maylin's grandpa have in his pocket?

b Why does Maylin want to have a cricket for a pet?

4 **Listen to the interview again.**

Fill in the missing words.

How to take care of a pet cricket

a Crickets need to stay _____. If you go out in winter, keep the cricket cage in a pocket, close to your body.

b Crickets need a safe _____, with plenty of air.

c Crickets need fresh _____ and water every day.

d Crickets can eat bits of rice and _____.

5 **What do you think?**

Different people like different things.
A cricket is a good pet for Maylin and her grandpa.

Is a cricket a good pet for you? Why or why not?

Write a few sentences.

A cricket is a good pet for me. I like to listen to crickets.

A cricket is not a good pet for me. My mum doesn't like insects.

❯ 6.3 Ants and spiders

We are going to...

- say how spiders and insects are similar and different.

1 **Look at the headings in Ants and Spiders.**

How are the headings similar?

What do you think you will learn about?

Ants

What does an ant look like?

An ant is an insect. It has six legs and two antennae.
Ants use their antennae to feel, smell and taste.
These ants are using their antennae to communicate.
What do you think they are saying?

Where do ants live?

Ants live in big groups. Some ants build homes with
many rooms under the ground.

What do ants eat?

Ants eat leaves, seeds, bugs and other things.
When ants go to find food, they leave a smell trail.
They carry their food home, following
their smell trail.

2 **What do you remember?**

Close your book. Tell your partner some
facts you remember about ants.

Then open the book. Read Ants again with
your partner. Find some more facts.

Key word

fact: a true piece
of information

71

3 **Listen and read about spiders.**

What is the most interesting fact?

Spiders

What does a spider look like?

Spiders are not insects. All spiders have eight legs. They don't have antennae or wings. Some spiders have eight eyes and some have six. But most spiders can't see very well!

Where do spiders live?

Some spiders live under the ground. Others make webs. A spider makes a web from silk in its body. The silk is very light and very strong.

What do spiders eat?

Most spiders eat insects. Some very big spiders eat mice and small fish too.

4 **Make your very own bug.**

Draw a picture or make a model of a make-believe bug.

Write about your bug. Answer these questions:

a   What is your bug's name?

b   What does it look like?

c   Where does it live?

d   What does it eat?

> 6.4 Writing questions

We are going to...

- write questions and answer them.

1 Ask and answer.

Read the information about **bees**. Then read the question and answer it.

Bees are helpful insects. They make honey.

People like eating honey.

Question: How do bees help people?

 Watch this!

2 Now answer questions about silkworms, crickets and butterflies.

Silkworms are helpful insects. They make silk.

People use silk to make beautiful clothes.

Question: How _____ silkworms help people?

Crickets don't have ears. They hear sounds through special spots on their legs.

Questions: Do crickets _____ ears?

How do crickets _____?

Butterflies don't have mouths. They taste food with their feet.

Questions: Do butterflies _____ _____?

How _____ butterflies _____ _____?

Language detective

What? Where? How?

Read the question and answer pairs.
Fill in the missing question word.

a   <u>Where</u> do you eat breakfast?   I eat breakfast at home.

b   _____ do you eat for breakfast?   I eat yogurt.

c   _____ do you eat yogurt?   I eat it with a spoon.

3   Make a game.

You are going to write questions for a game.

Look at the facts on pages 100, 101 and 102.
Write three questions starting with:

What do ...?   Where do ...?   How do ...?
How many ...?   Do ...?

- Write each question on a card.
- On the back of the card draw 1 star ⭐ for an easy question or 2 stars ⭐⭐ for a hard question.
- Give your cards to your teacher.

4   Play the game.

Play in two teams.

Teams take turns choosing an easy or a hard question.

You score like this:

- **2 points** for answering a hard question
- **1 point** for answering an easy question
- **0 point** for a wrong answer.

> 6.5 Rhyming words, words with long e

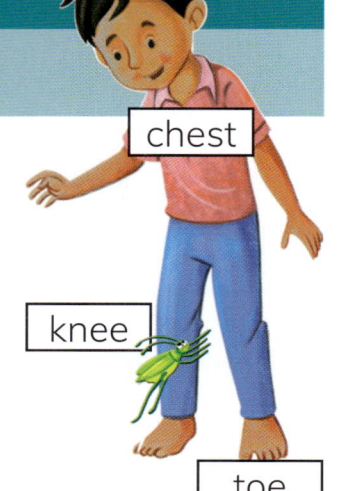

head

chest

knee

toe

We are going to...

- read and write words with the spelling **ee** and **ea**.

 1 Find the rhyming word.

Where is the cricket?

Each missing word rhymes with the word in red.
Use words from the picture.

Oh no, oh **no**!

There's a cricket on my _____.

Oh poor, poor **me**.

There's a cricket on my _____.

Oh, this cricket's such a **pest**!

Now it's sitting on my _____.

Did you hear what I **said**?

There's a cricket on my _____.

 2 Listen, point and sing!

There's a cricket on the floor.
There's a cricket on the floor, on the floor.
There's a cricket on the floor, on the floor.
Now it's coming through the door,
That cricket on the floor.
There's a cricket on the floor, on the floor.

Now the cricket's on my **toe**, on my **toe**.
Now the cricket's on my **knee**, on my **knee**.
Now the cricket's on my **chest**, on my **chest**.
Now the cricket's on my **head**, on my **head**.
Now there's a cricket on the floor, on the floor.

3   Long e spellings

Say and write these words. What vowel sound do they all have?

knee   flea   me   bee   she   leaf   feet   eat

Underline the letters in each word that stand for the long **e** sound.

4   Take a spelling quiz.

Ask your partner to spell three of
the long **e** words. Then switch.

How do you
spell **bee**?

b - e - e.

5   Sticker activity

 Sometimes **ea** makes
the long **e** sound: **eat**

 Sometimes **ea** makes the
short **e** sound: **head**

cheese   tea   bread   meat

Read the words. Find the stickers.

Which words have the long **e** sound?
Which words have the letters **ea**? Which word has the short **e** sound?

Put the stickers on the Food page (page 170) of the Picture dictionary.

6   Listen to the poem.

Which words have the long **e** sound? Write the words in a list.

Which words have the short **e** sound?
Write the words in a second list.

A bee and a flea
Had breakfast with tea.
The bee bumped his head
And went back to bed.

> 6.6 Little Ant

We are going to...

- read, discuss and act out a story.

1 Before you read

Look at the pictures to get information.

Who are the characters in this story?

What do you think happens in the story?

Now, read the story to find if your answers are correct!

> **Reading tip**
>
> This story is a folktale from Mexico.

Little Ant

It was a chilly autumn day.
Little Ant said, 'I'm going out to play.'
'Come home soon,' said her mother. 'It's getting cold outside.
But our home under the ground is nice and warm.'

Little Ant met a beetle and a worm.
'Hello,' said Little Ant. 'Let's play!'
'OK,' said the beetle and the worm.
They played and played together.

The wind began to **blow**.
Little Ant began to **shiver**.
'It's cold,' she said. 'I have to
go home.'

Little Ant started to walk home.
The wind blew harder and Little Ant shivered.
A big leaf fell on her.
'Help!' said Little Ant. 'I can't move!'

'Leaf, please get off me,' said Little Ant.
'I have to go home.'
But the leaf didn't move.

Little Ant called to a mouse.
'Mouse, mouse, can you help me?
Please **lift up** the leaf.
It's cold and I have to go home.'

But the mouse said, 'Sorry, Little Ant.
I can't help you now. I am very busy.'

So Little Ant called to a cat.
'Cat, cat, can you help me?
Please **chase** the mouse.
Mouse, please lift up the leaf.
It's cold and I have to go home.'

But the cat said, 'Sorry, Little Ant.
I can't help you now. I am very busy.'

So Little Ant called to a dog.
'Dog, dog, can you help me?
Please **scare** the cat.

Cat, please chase the mouse.
Mouse, please lift up the leaf.
It's cold and I have to go home.'

But the dog said, 'Sorry, Little Ant.
I can't help you now. I am very busy.'

A flea who lived on the dog
heard Little Ant calling for help.
The flea is a cousin of the ant.

'Don't worry, Cousin Ant,' called the flea.
'I can help you. I'll **bite** this dog.'
So the flea bit the dog.

The dog yelped and scared the cat.

The cat turned and chased the mouse.

The mouse ran to Little Ant and lifted up the leaf.

'Thank you, Cousin Flea!' called Little Ant.

Little Ant ran back to her nice, warm
home under the ground.
'I'm back, Mum!' Little Ant called.
'Hello, Little Ant,' said her mother.
'I am glad you're home!'

2   Find these verbs in the story.

blow   shiver   lift up   chase   scare   bite

Talk about their meaning and take turns acting out the words for your partner to guess.

Then find the past simple form of each verb in the story.

3   Values: Being helpful

Everyone needs a little help sometimes. In the story, who needs help?

Which character is helpful? Which characters are not helpful?

Think of a time that you were helpful. Tell your partner about it.

4   Story map

A story often begins with a problem and ends with a solution.

🔒 The problem	🔑 The solution
A big leaf falls on Little Ant. Little Ant can't move. The mouse, the cat and the dog will not help her.	How did the problem get fixed? It started with Cousin Flea. Look at the pictures on page 108. Retell that part of the story 1 Cousin Flea ___bit___ the dog. 2 The dog _____ the cat. 3 The cat _____. 4 The mouse _____. 5 Little Ant _____.

5   Act it out!

Make puppets and act out the story of Little Ant.

› 6.7 Project challenge

Work on the project with a partner or group. Then share with the class.

A: Write bug riddles

- Write riddles about bugs.

- Draw pictures or find photos.

- Your classmates must match the riddles with the pictures.

I have 4 short legs
and 2 long legs.
Who am I?

I make silk.
Who am I?

76

B: Perform a life cycle poem

- Learn about the life cycle of a caterpillar.
  Look up information in books or on the Internet.

- Draw a life cycle diagram.

- Practise reading the poem aloud.
  Make up actions to go with the words.

- Perform the poem for your class. Share your life cycle diagram.

Fuzzy little caterpillar
Into a corner will creep.
She'll spin herself a blanket
And then go fast asleep.
Fuzzy little caterpillar
Will wake up by and by,
To find she has grown a pair of wings.
Now she's a butterfly!

butterfly
caterpillar
chrysalis

C: Draw and write a cartoon story

Your story will compare a boy and an insect.

How are they the same? How are they different?

Write the words in speech bubbles.

How did you help share your project with the class?

Look what I can do!

- I can read and talk about insects.
- I can learn about insects.
- I can say how spiders and insects are similar and different.
- I can write questions and answer them.
- I can read and write words with the spelling ee and ea.
- I can read, discuss and act out a story.

> ## Check your progress 2
Last year and yesterday

You need:

- 2 to 3 players
- a different game marker for each player
- number cards.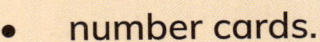

Directions

- Take a number card.
- Count and move your game marker on the game track.
- Read and answer the questions.
- Read and follow the directions.
- Name the picture. Use the word in a sentence.

16

15
Where were you last night?

14
Find an animal with 8 legs.

13
Find a heavy animal.

12

START →

1
What did you eat yesterday?

2
Find a picture that rhymes with spoon.

3
How old were you last year?

⟩ 7.1 Caring for planet Earth

We are going to...

- talk about caring for planet Earth.

Getting started

How can we care for planet Earth?

77 1 **Listen and say.**

Su Lyn and her family are celebrating Mother Earth Day.

What are they doing?

What will they do every day?

Watch this!

2 **Listen, point, and say.**

planting   watering   picking up   bin   recycle

 3 **Listen to Su Lyn again.**

Then finish the sentences.

a   Dad is planting trees with _____.

b   Mum is counting birds with _____.

c   My brother is picking up litter with _____.

d   My cousin is making paper flowers with _____.

his friends   my aunt   my uncle   my grandma

 4 **Listen, read and act out the poem.**

I'm glad the sky is painted blue
And Earth is painted green,
With such a lot of nice fresh air
All sandwiched in between.

> 7.2 Plants and flowers

We are going to...

- **learn about plants.**

1   Grow some plants in your classroom.

Outside, the green leaves of trees clean the dirty air.
They give us fresh air to breathe.

Green plants can help clean the air inside too.
Grow some plants in your classroom.
Watch your plants grow and change.
Draw diagrams. Measure your growing plant.
Count the leaves and flowers.

water — — marbles
or pebbles

2   Sticker activity

Label the parts of the
plant in this diagram.

roots   stem

leaf   flower

3 Listen and write.

What do you love about planet Earth? Discuss.

Listen to this poem. Then write your own poem.

A poem for Mother Earth

Earth is my home.

I love the tall trees,

The soft wind,

The smell of flowers and grass,

The sound of birds in the morning.

I will take care of Earth.

4 Make a paper flower.

You need: a stack of 4 to 6 pieces of tissue paper and a pipe cleaner.

1 Fold the paper. Turn the paper over. Fold again. Turn the paper over. Repeat. Your paper will look like a staircase. 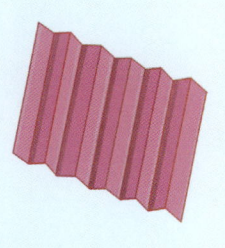	2 Wrap a pipe cleaner around the middle. 
3 Use your fingers. Separate each layer of paper. 	4 Who is your flower for? Write a gift tag. 

> 7.3 The importance of trees

We are going to...

- **learn about trees and recycling.**

Key word

wood

81   **1**   **Listen and read.**

What are some 'gifts' we get from trees?

Name five things. Then listen and read to learn more.

Gifts from trees

Can you think of a fruit that grows on a tree?
Apples, mangoes, cherries and many other
fruits do. Nuts grow on trees too.

People and animals eat the fruit and
nuts of trees. Trees are also homes
for many animals, including birds,
monkeys, frogs, lizards and snakes.

Disappearing trees

All over the world, people are cutting down trees.
People cut down trees to make room for new buildings.
They cut down trees to get more **wood**.
People use wood to make fires for cooking and warmth.
They use wood to build houses and boats and furniture.
They use wood to make paper.

When trees are cut down, animals lose their homes.
There are fewer trees to clean the air.

How many animals
are in this tree?

118 >

Help save the trees!

Huge numbers of trees are cut down every day.

Forests are disappearing.

How can children help?

In some schools, children plant trees.

In many schools, children try to use less paper.

They write on both sides of each piece of paper.

They put used paper in a recycling box.

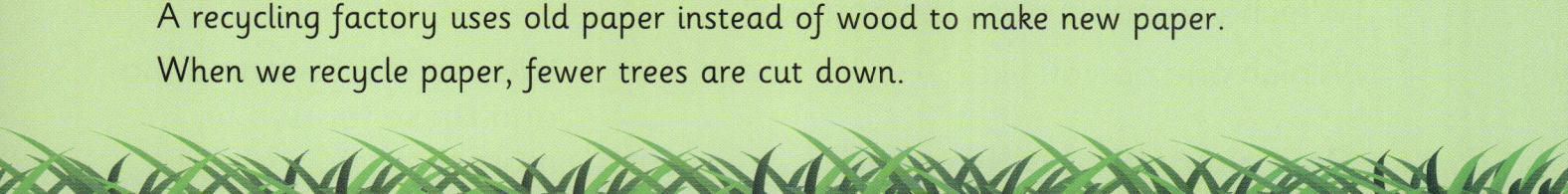

A recycling factory uses old paper instead of wood to make new paper.

When we recycle paper, fewer trees are cut down.

2   Find the matching pictures.

What can you make from recycled paper?

cards   boxes   magazines   paper towels   nappies

3   Talk about it.

Look around the classroom.
Name all the things that are made from wood.
(Don't forget that paper is made from wood!)

> 7.4 Using *this* and *these*, *that* and *those*

We are going to...

- role-play conversations at a market.

 1 **Choosing a plant**

A little boy and his dad are choosing a vegetable plant at the market.

Listen and point.
Which vegetable does the boy like?

Which one do you like?

Language tip

We use **this** for one thing and **these** for two or more things.

We use **that** for one thing and **those** for two or more things.

2 **Role play: What is this plant?**

Pretend you are the boy in the picture.
Point to a plant or a group of plants.
Ask a question. Your partner will answer.

What is this plant?

This is a potato plant.

What are these plants?

These are onion plants.

3 **What do you do first?**

Tell the little boy how to take care of his plant.
Work with a partner.
Put the picture cards in the right order.
Write the 4 direction steps.

1 First, dig a hole.
2 Next, _____.
3 Next, _____.
4 Then, _____.

water the plant

dig a hole

fill the hole with soil

put the plant in the hole

4 **Listen.**

What fruit does the woman buy?
Now read and fill in the missing words.

 Hello! Can I have two _____, please?

Of course! Are _____ OK?

Yes, thank you. Those are great.

Anything else?

Yes. A pineapple, _____.

How about _____ one?

Yes, _____ one looks nice. Thank you.

You're welcome.

> mangoes   that
> please   these
>   this

Language detective

Fill in the missing word using **that** or **these**.

We use **this** and _____ for things that are very near to us.

We use _____ and **those** for things that are less near.

5 **Role play: At the fruit stand**

Make a fruit stand.

Draw, colour, cut out and make signs for your favourite fruits.
Then role-play buying and selling fruit.

> I'd like two pears, please.

> Are these OK?

> 7.5 Long **o**

We are going to...

- say and write words with long o spellings.

 1 **Listen, point and sing!**

Look at the words in the picture.
Which words have a long **o** sound?

> Holding hands out in the snow
> Slowly on our way we go
> Leaving little paths behind
> For the winter owl to find.

 2 **Listen and write the words.**

All the words have the long **o** sound.

Work with a partner. Say the words. Find the matching picture.

Underline the letters that make the long **o** sound.

a    b 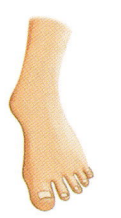   c    d

e    f    g    h

3 **Sticker activity**

Sometimes **ow** makes the long **o** sound: sn**ow**

Sometimes **ow** makes a different sound: **ow**l

Read the words. Find the stickers.

owl	crow	cow

Which word has the long **o** sound?

Put them on the Animals page (page 173) of the Picture dictionary.

 4 **Read and listen to the poem.**

Act out the words! Then look for words with the letters **ow**.

In which words do the letters **ow** make the long **o** sound?

In which words do the letters **ow** make the sound you hear in **c**ow?

Work with a partner. Write two lists.

Sounds of ow	
cr**ow**	**c**ow

Five little seeds

Under the leaves,
And under the snow,
Five little seeds are
Waiting to grow.

Out comes the sun,
Down comes a shower.
And up come five
Pretty pink flowers.

› 7.6 Wangari Maathai

We are going to…

- **read and discuss a biography.**

1 **Look at the title and the pictures.**

Why do you think Wangari is famous?

2 **Read to find out why Wangari is called 'Mama Trees'.**

Wangari Maathai: 'Mama Trees'

Wangari Maathai was born in 1940 in a small village in Kenya. Green trees covered the land. Families grew food in small gardens. A little river brought clean water to the village. Women and children picked figs and other fruit from the trees. The families used wood to make fires for cooking. Wangari loved her green and beautiful home.

When Wangari grew older, she went away to school. She studied in the United States and in Germany.

When Wangari came back to Kenya, the land
looked very different. The trees were gone.
Without the trees, the sun had dried the earth.
The family garden was gone.
The little river was dry.

The people in Wangari's village now had to walk
a long way to get clean water and firewood.

Wangari felt very sad. What could she do to help?
An idea came to her. She would plant trees.
Kenya could become green and beautiful again.

Wangari took seeds from trees.
She planted the seeds in her garden.
She watered them every day.
The seeds grew into little trees.

Wangari gave the little trees to the women and children in her village. Together they planted rows and rows of little trees. Every day, the women and children watered the trees. The trees grew.

Soon there were figs and other fruits to eat.
There was clean water in the little rivers.
There was wood for homes and fires.
'When we plant trees, we plant the seeds of peace and hope,' said Wangari.

People all over Africa learned from Wangari.
They planted millions of trees. Wangari became very famous. People called her 'Mama Trees.'
'Little things make a big difference,' said Wangari.
'My little thing is planting trees.'

3 **What happened first? What happened next?**

Work with a partner. Put these sentences in the correct order.

____ Wangari watered the seeds every day.
They grew into little trees.

_1_ Wangari took seeds from trees.
She planted the seeds in her garden.

____ The trees grew big. Fruit grew on the trees.

____ Wangari gave the little trees to women and
children in her village.

____ Together they planted many rows of trees.

4 **Values: Little things can make a big difference.**

What 'little thing' did Wangari do? How did it make a big difference?

Think of a little thing that someone did that made you feel happy.

Share a story of a little thing.

Then, talk about a 'little thing' that you could do
that would make someone else happy.

5 **Write your autobiography.**

An autobiography is the story of your own life.

In your autobiography, write:

- where you were born
- two interesting things that have happened to you
- how old you were when each thing happened
- what you would like to do when you grow up.

> 7.7 Project challenge

Work on the project with a partner or group. Then share with the class.

A: Make a poster: Be kind to our planet

Think of some nice things you can do for planet Earth.

- You can put litter in a bin.
- You can recycle bottles.

What else can you do?

Make a poster with your ideas.

Try to make your poster on recycled cardboard or paper!

Be kind to our planet. Grow a plant!

B: Make a book about your heroes

Wangari Maathai is a hero to many people. She made the world a better place.

Think of someone you know who makes the world a better place.

- Maybe they help people or animals?
- Maybe they help keep your town or school safe?
- Maybe they make beautiful things?

My grandma is my hero. She cares for all the children.

Make a book with your friends.

Write about a different hero on each page.

Each person must write a page about their hero.

C: Our national tree, flower and bird

What's the national flower or animal of your country?

How can you find out?

Make a poster or a slideshow that shows the national tree, flower and animal of your country.

You can use photos or draw pictures.

Choose a second country.

Make a poster or a slideshow that shows the national tree, flower and bird of that country.

Malaysia

Our national tree is the merbau tree.
It is very tall!
Our national flower is the bunga raya.
Our national bird is the rhinoceros hornbill.

What is something you learned from another group's project?

Look what I can do!

- I can talk about caring for planet Earth.
- I can learn about plants.
- I can learn about trees and recycling.
- I can role-play conversations at a market.
- I can read and write words with long o spellings.
- I can read and discuss a biography.

8 ▶ Home, sweet home

❭ 8.1 Different kinds of homes

We are going to...

- talk and write about different kinds of homes.

Getting started

What different kinds of homes are there?

1 **Listen to Mia talk about the tree house.**

How do you get to the second floor?

Can all the children go there?

2 **Listen, point, and say.**

Then answer the questions.

roof   wall   stairs   ladder   railing   basket

3 **What can you see in the picture?**

Read the questions and talk with your partner.
Share your answers with the class.

a   What animals and animal homes do you see in the picture?

b   Name some animals that live in a tree.

c   Name some animals that live in a hole.

4 **Read and listen to the poem.**

Homes

A nest is a home for a bird.

A hive is a home for a bee.

A hole is a home for a rabbit.

And a house is a home for me.

5 **Write your own poem.**

Work with a partner.

Your poem can be about homes for animals or homes for things!

Look at the poem above about homes.

Then write your own version of the poem with your own ideas.

A sock is a home for a foot.

A shelf is a home for a book.

A cup is a home for milk or for tea.

And a house is a home for for me.

❯ 8.2 Inside a home

We are going to...

• **talk about things we do at home.**

 1 **Listen and point to the picture of Kevin's home.**

What does he do when he comes home from school?

Use your finger to show where Kevin goes.

 2 **Listen again to find the answers.**

    a Where does he put his shoes and jacket?

    b Where does he put his backpack?

    c Where does he wash his hands?

    d Where does he eat his snack?

Kevin's bedroom

Hall

Kitchen

Garden

Bathroom

3 **Talk with your partner.**

When you get home, where do you put your things?

| shoes | jacket | school uniform | backpack |

4 **Sticker activity**

Sort the stickers. In which room does each thing belong?

bed	sink	toilet

kitchen	bathroom	bedroom

5 **What's in your room?**

Draw a room in your home and write a description.

How many windows are in the room?

What furniture is in the room?

There are 2 windows in my bedroom.
There is a bed, a rug and a toy box.
There is a teddy bear on my bed.

6 **What does Loni do at home?**

Listen, point to the pictures below and say the words.

Then listen to Loni talk about the things she does.

Which things does she not do?

wash my hands

brush my teeth

set the table

put dishes in the sink

tidy my room

make my bed

sweep the floor

put my clean clothes away

7 **How about you?**

Which things do you do at home?

Tell your partner.
Then, ask your classmates questions.

Ravi, do you make your bed?

> 8.3 Homes around the world

We are going to...

- **read about different kinds of homes.**

1 **Before you read**

What is the weather like where you live?

Do you have houses like these in your country?

Adobe house in Ghana

Different kinds of homes

Adobe houses

In some **hot**, dry places, people build houses made from mud and dry grass. These are called adobe houses. The thick mud walls keep the houses **cool**.

Stilt houses

In some hot, wet places, people build houses on stilts. Stilt houses are built high above the water or land. The 'stilts' are tree trunks. The air blows under the houses and keeps them cool.

Cave houses

Cave homes are built in rocky cliffs. Cave homes stay cool during the summer. They stay **warm** during the **cold** winter.

Stilt house in Borneo

Cave house in Turkey

Key words

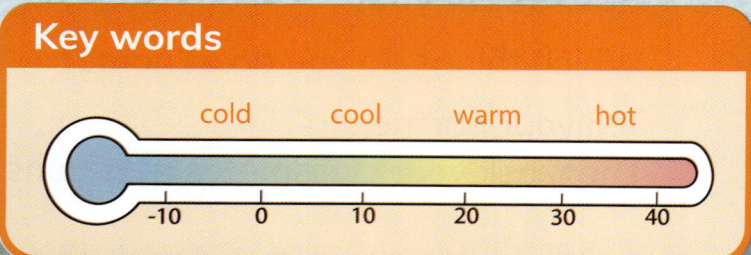

cold	cool	warm	hot
-10	0	10 20	30 40

Skyscrapers

In cities all over the world, people live in tall buildings called skyscrapers. Skyscrapers are made of metal, concrete and glass. This skyscraper has more than 160 floors and 57 lifts!

Burj Khalifa skyscraper in Dubai

2   True or false?

Choose **true** or **false** for each statement.

a   Adobe houses have thick walls made of mud and dry grass.   **True   False**

b   Stilt houses keep you warm in cold weather.   **True   False**

c   People dig into rock to make a cave house.   **True   False**

d   A skyscraper has lots of windows.   **True   False**

3   How does your home keep you cool in hot weather?

How does it keep you warm when the weather is cold?

Discuss these questions with your partner.

4   Where do they live?

Read the clues. Where does each child live?

a      To get to my home, I go up in a lift.

b      To get to my home, I ride in a boat.

c      I live in a hot place, but inside my house it is cool.

d   My bedroom is inside a mountain!

135 〉

> 8.4 Using future form *will*

We are going to...

- **talk about things in the future using *will*.**

> Will we have a tunnel or a bridge?

1   How do you plan a playground?

These children are going to have a new playground!

The playground designer is asking them what they want.

Listen and point to the things that the children choose.

straight slide   **curvy slide**   **rope ladder**   **metal ladder**

swings   **hoops**   **see-saw**   **merry-go-round**

2   What will you have in your playground?

Work with a partner.

Design your own playground!

Draw pictures and glue them on a piece of paper.

Then write a description of your playground.

Our Playground

Our playground will have 2 slides and 5 swings. It will have a merry-go-round too.

3 Experiment: Will it slide?

Make a slide using a book and a piece of cardboard.

Place a **paper clip** at the top of the slide. Does it slide down the slide?

What if you make the slide steeper?

Add one more book. Do you think the paper clip will slide? Make a prediction.

Write your prediction on the chart. Then try it out!

Write the result on the chart.

Will the paper clip slide with 2 books?

Yes, it will.

No, it won't.

Did the paper clip slide?

Yes, it did.

No, it didn't.

If the paper clip <u>didn't</u> slide, add one more book.

Make a prediction, then try it out.

Do the same experiment with a **coin** and a **pencil**.

Write your predictions and your results on a chart.

Compare the three charts. What do you notice?

Language detective

Write the missing word. Use these letters: **o t w n**

will not =

___ ___ ___ , ___

Will the paper clip slide? 📎		
	Make a prediction.	**Try it out! Did it slide?**
2 books	Yes, it will.	No, it didn't.
3 books	No, it won't.	No, it didn't.
4 books	Yes, it will.	
5 books		
6 books		
7 books		

> 8.5 Long *u* and **oo**

We are going to...

- **read and write words with long *u* and *oo* spellings.**

95 **1 Let's build a cool house!**

Listen and read these instructions.
Look at the words in **red**.

What sound do you hear in these words?

> **You** can build a **cool** house with boxes.
> **You** will need sticky tape, **glue** and scissors.
> **Use** some tubes **too**.
> Will your house have one **room** or a **few** rooms?

Find words above that rhyme with **zoo**.
The vowel sound has different spellings.

Find words where the vowel has the same spelling as:

zoo   **blue**   **grew**

96 **2 The sounds of oo**

The letters **oo** stand for the vowel sound
in **too** and **zoo**. Listen to these words:

goose   **moon**   **roof**   **food**

Then use them to talk about the picture.

Sometimes, the letters **oo** stand for a
different sound.

Listen and say these words:

wood   **foot**   **book**   **look**

Use these words to talk about the picture.

3 **Sticker activity**

Sometimes **oo** makes the sound you hear in **zoo**.

Sometimes **oo** makes a different sound: **book**.

Read the words. Find the stickers.
Which two words have the sound you hear in **zoo**?

roof	bedroom	cooker

Put the stickers on the Home page (page 168) of the Picture dictionary.

What can you find in a home that is not on the Picture dictionary page?

4 **Listen, sing and point.**

Let's build a house

Let's build a house
We'll start with a floor,
Add walls and windows
And, of course, a door.

A roof on top with a chimney tall
And outside the house, a garden wall.

A table and umbrella for a sunny day.
A pretty little garden where we can play.

5 **Make a pop-up paper house.**

Colour the house. Draw a garden.

Fold the paper in half.

Cut on the thick lines.

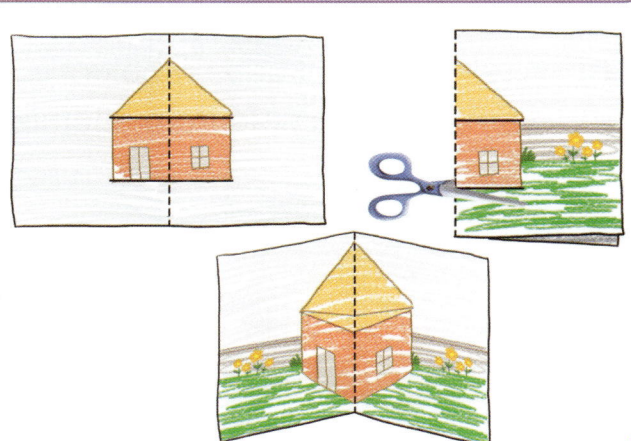

8.6 Where do animals build homes?

We are going to...

- **read and discuss informational text.**

1   Before you read

Work together in a group of three – one of you will read *Rabbit homes*, one will read *Termite homes* and one will read *Beaver homes*. Then the three of you will talk and share what you have learned.

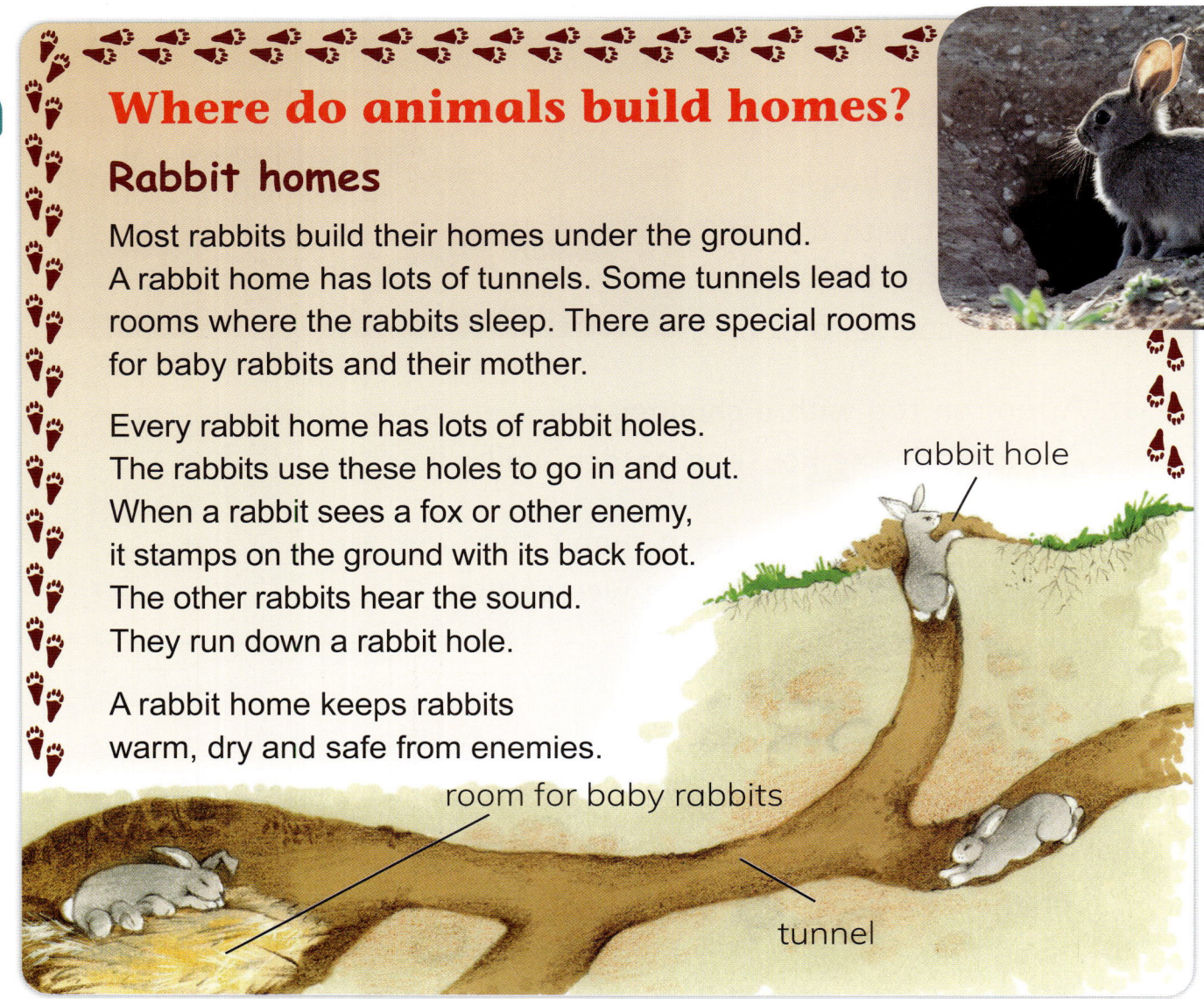

Where do animals build homes?

Rabbit homes

Most rabbits build their homes under the ground. A rabbit home has lots of tunnels. Some tunnels lead to rooms where the rabbits sleep. There are special rooms for baby rabbits and their mother.

Every rabbit home has lots of rabbit holes. The rabbits use these holes to go in and out. When a rabbit sees a fox or other enemy, it stamps on the ground with its back foot. The other rabbits hear the sound. They run down a rabbit hole.

A rabbit home keeps rabbits warm, dry and safe from enemies.

rabbit hole

room for baby rabbits

tunnel

98

Termite homes

Tiny insects called termites build tall towers from mud. The towers can be over 2 metres tall! You can find these tall termite towers in Australia, Africa and South America. The termites live in the towers and in the ground below.

The termites' home has lots of tunnels and rooms.
In the middle of the home, there is a room for the queen. The queen lays eggs.

Some termites build rooms that are gardens. They grow a special mushroom in these gardens. The termites eat these mushrooms.

The termites build air holes to keep their home cool when the weather is hot.

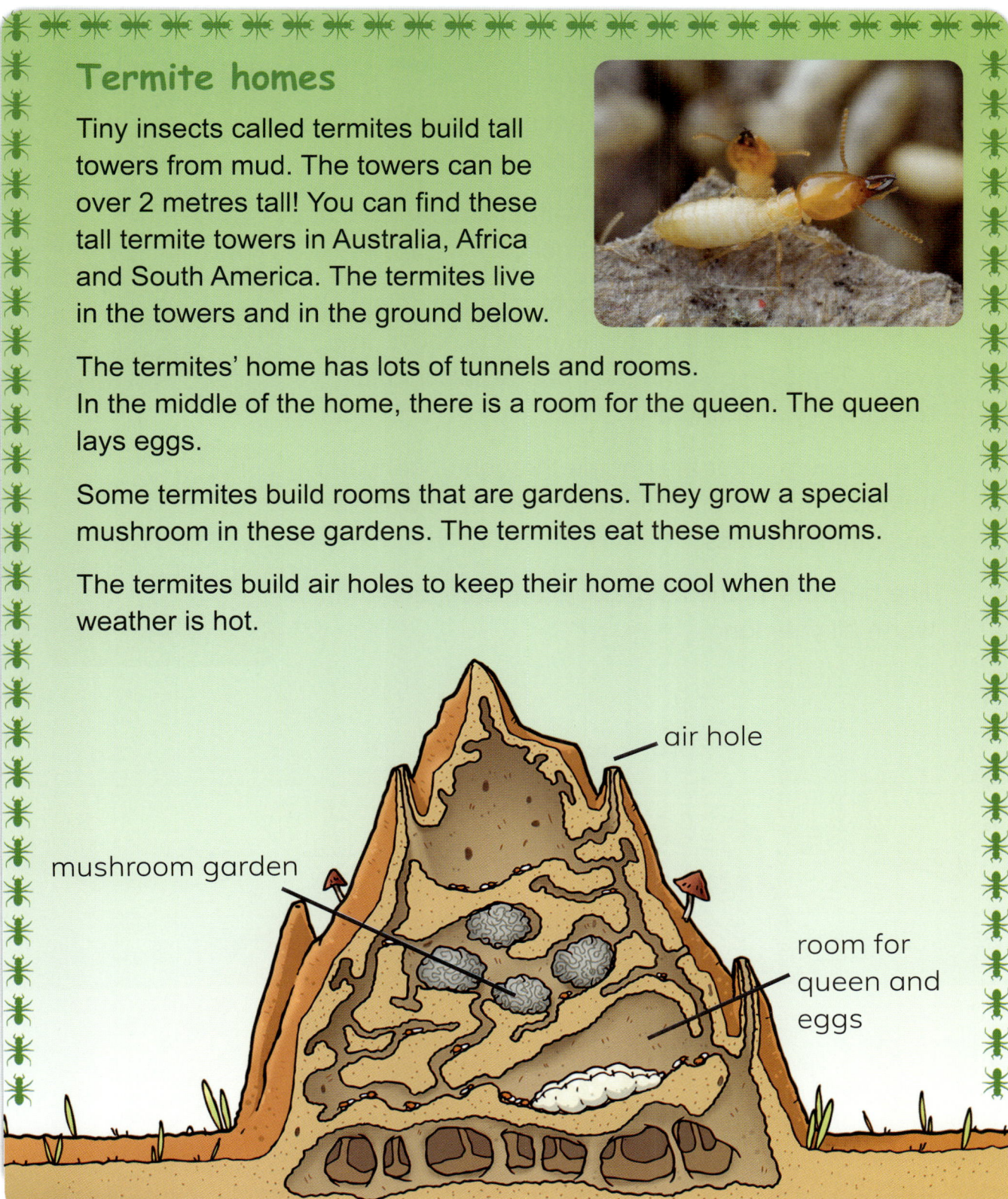

air hole

mushroom garden

room for queen and eggs

141 >

Beaver homes

Beavers build homes from branches, rocks and mud. They build their homes in the middle of a pond.

The beavers cut down trees with their sharp teeth. They make a huge pile of branches.

The beavers build one big room in the middle of their home. The floor of the room is above the water. The beavers and their babies live in this room. It is warm and dry.

The beavers enter their home through underwater tunnels. This keeps their home safe from wolves and other enemies.

The beavers' home keeps beavers safe, dry and warm all year long.

branches, rock and mud

underground tunnel

2 **Share your information.**

Meet in your team of three. Answer these questions about **rabbits**, **termites** and **beavers**. Point to the diagram of the animal's home as you share what you learned.

I learned about rabbit homes.

I learned about termite homes.

I learned about beaver homes.

a Where does your animal build its home?

b Does it have one room or many rooms?

c Are there special rooms in the home? Talk about those rooms.

d Why is the home a good home for the animal?

3 **Which animal home?**

Answer these questions with your team.

a Which animal home has a garden inside? What grows in the garden?

b Which animal home has a room built above water? Is the room wet or dry?

c Which animal stamps its foot when it sees a fox? What happens then?

4 **Values: Working together**

In this lesson, each person read about a different animal home, and then shared the information they learned.

Think of some others projects and games where you have been part of a team. What are some examples of things that are better or more fun when you work together? Write a list!

143

> 8.7 Project challenge

Work on the project with a partner or group. Then share with the class.

A: Write about an animal home

Choose an animal. Look up information about that animal's home in a book or on the Internet.

Where does the animal build its home?

What is the home made of?

Find some other interesting facts about the home.

Draw a diagram. Add word labels to the diagram.

ant

owl

turtle

monkey

spider

mouse

B: Design a playroom for children

What will you put in the playroom?

You could put: a huge TV, a ping-pong table, ropes and slides.

What else?

Draw a big picture of the room. Write word labels on the objects in the room.

television

slide

ladder

C: Doors in our school

Take photos or draw pictures of at least 5 different doors in your school such as a door to a room, a cupboard door or the front door of the school.

Write a card with this information about each door:

- Where is this door?
- What is this door made of: wood or metal?
- Does this door have a door knob?
- Is there a window or a number on this door?

Make a poster with all your door pictures and number them.

Read out your descriptions and let the class guess the doors.

This is a door to a cupboard.

It is made of wood.

It has a doorknob.

It is in our classroom.

What would you do differently if you were to do this project again?

Look what I can do!

I can talk and write about different kinds of homes.	○	○
I can talk about things I do at home.	○	○
I can read about different kinds of homes.	○	○
I can talk about things in the future, using *will*.	○	○
I can read and write words with long *u* spellings.	○	○
I can read and discuss informational text.	○	○

9 > Let's explore the city!

> 9.1 Things in a city

We are going to...

- talk about city things and places.

Getting started

What can you see and do in a city?

Look at the picture for more ideas.

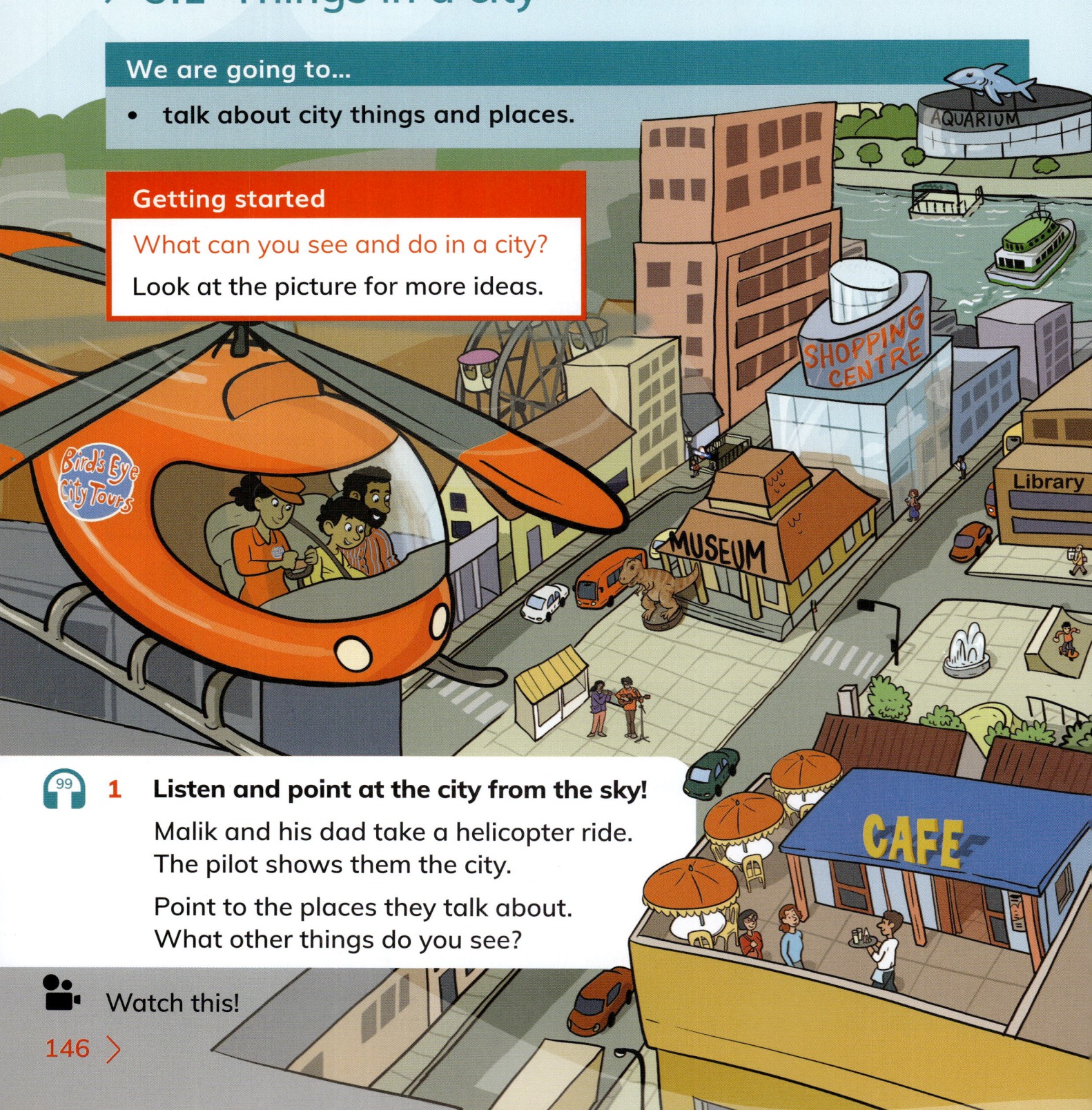

1 Listen and point at the city from the sky!

Malik and his dad take a helicopter ride. The pilot shows them the city.

Point to the places they talk about. What other things do you see?

Watch this!

2 **Listen, point and say.**

Listen to the sounds of the city and answer the questions.

What is making each sound?
Point and say the word.

traffic   helicopter   ferry   musicians   underground train

3 **I do too!**

Sometimes Dad and Malik like the same things and sometimes they do not!

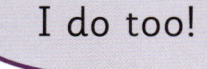 I like looking at sharks.   I do too!

I like shopping.   I don't!

riding on the underground

visiting the library

flying in a helicopter

looking at sharks

With a partner, take turns saying one thing you like.

The other person will say, **I do too!** or **I don't**.

going on a ferry

riding on a Ferris wheel

 4 **Read and listen to the poem.**

At the zebra crossing
Look around at city places.
Look around at city faces.
I bend down to tie my laces ... Oops!
WALK! Hurry up! Let's cross!

> 9.2 At the aquarium

We are going to...

- use describing words.

1 **Sticker activity**

What's happening at the aquarium today? Look at the poster and listen to the announcement. Put the stickers in the correct place.

octopus   jellyfish   penguin   sea turtle

Meet our amazing animals

10:00
They're clever!

11:00
They're beautiful!

12:00
They're hungry!

1:00
They're huge!

2 **Read the describing words.**

Read the words aloud and talk about their meaning.

Then listen to the audio again. Which words do you hear?

amazing   beautiful   clever   clumsy   cute   dangerous
fast   gentle   graceful   huge   little   scary   strange

3 **Describe a mystery animal.**

Work with a partner. Choose an aquarium animal. Write a description of the animal, but don't write its name! Can your classmates guess the animal?

It has big teeth.
It is scary and dangerous.
It can swim. It has fins.
It doesn't have legs.

4 **Listen and write.**

Sami and Nasima are in the aquarium shop.

What do you think they will buy?

Listen to the conversation. Fill in the missing words.

Here	or
penguins	please
with	

Boy: Hello. Can I have **that** hat, _____?

Seller: The one with the turtle?

Boy: No, the one _____ the shark.

Seller: Here you are.

Boy: Thank you.

Girl: Can I have **those** gloves, please?

Seller: The ones with the _____?

Girl: Yes, that's right.

Seller: Do you want the red gloves _____ the grey gloves?

Girl: The red ones, please.

Seller: _____ you are.

5 **Role play with a partner.**

Practise the conversation. What will you buy?

Can I have those **socks**, please?

The ones with the **alligators**?

> 9.3 Going places

We are going to...

- **follow and give directions**

 104

1   Follow directions.

Look at the city map.
Listen to the conversations.

Use your finger on the map to follow the directions.

 105

2   Where are you?

Listen. Use your finger on the map and follow the directions. Where are you?

Choose the correct answer.

Riverside Café
Shopping Centre
Museum
Library
Skate park

Excuse me. Where is the skate park?

Walk straight ahead. The skate park is on the right.

at the shopping centre	at the Riverside Café
at the market	at the museum

3   Direct your partner around the map.

Work with a partner. Choose a place on the map.

Give your partner directions to get there.

Use the map and some of the phrases below.

Walk straight ahead.   **Take the first left.**

Go up to the traffic light.   **Walk to the next street.**

Turn right.   **It's on your left.**

4   At the Riverside Café

Look at the menu. Listen to Rosa and her dad talking to the waiter.

What do they order to eat and to drink?

Menu
Things to eat
pizza
fish and chips
noodle soup
chicken sandwich
salad

Things to drink
strawberry smoothie
pear juice
sparkling water
apple juice
milk

5   Over to you!

Role-play with a partner. One of you will be the waiter.
The other will order something to eat and drink.
Here are some things you can say.

Can I take your order, please?

Yes, can I have _____?

Of course. And something to drink?

_____, please.

6   Strawberry smoothies

Try this recipe for strawberry smoothies!

Make a recipe for your own favourite smoothie.

You can use different fruit and different juice.

Strawberry smoothie

1 frozen banana
8 strawberries
100 ml orange juice
100 ml yogurt

1 Cut the banana in pieces.
2 Put the bananas, strawberries, orange juice and yogurt in a blender.
3 Blend and drink!

> 9.4 The past, present and future

We are going to...

- **talk and write about activities in the past, present and future.**

 1   A great day today! A great day tomorrow!

Read the brochure, which describes 6 great things kids can do in the city.

Listen to a brother and sister talk about what they did in the city today and what they will do tomorrow.

Fill in the chart. Did they do it today or will they do it tomorrow?

Today	Tomorrow
skateboarding	

2 **Write and draw.**

Pretend you are the brother or sister you heard on the audio.

Write a postcard telling a friend what you did in the city today and what you will do tomorrow.

Use the notes you wrote on the Today/Tomorrow chart.

Draw a picture of a city place you wrote about on the other side of your postcard.

Language detective

Which sentence tells about something that happened in the past?

Which sentence tells about something that will happen in the future?

How do you know?

We ate at the Rooftop Café.

Tomorrow, we will ride a Ferris wheel!

3 **What are you doing now?**

Pretend you are having fun in the city. What are you doing? Choose an activity from the brochure. Write a sentence on a strip of paper.

As a class, sort the sentence strips into piles. Then tape each pile together into one long strip.

Which strip is the longest?
This is the winner – the activity your class likes the best!

I am visiting the zoo.

I am watching a puppet show.

I am riding the Ferris wheel. I am riding the Ferris wheel. I am riding the Ferris wheel.

> 9.5 Opposites

We are going to...

- use opposite words.

YES   NO

 1 **Listen, sing and act it out.**

Half of the class will sing the red words.
Half of the class will sing the blue words.

Everyone will sing the **black** words.

Opposites

When I say **day**,
I say **night**.
When I say **black**,
I say **white**.
When I go **left**,
I go **right**.
We're opposites!
When I say **yes**,
I say **no**.
When I say '**Stop**!'
I say, '**Go**!'
When I sing **high**,
I sing **low**.

Chorus

We're opposites, you and me.
We're different as can **be**.
We always **disagree**. Opposites!

I sit.
I **stand**.

But we go hand in **hand**
On water or on **land**.
Opposites!

you are here

When I'm **lost**,
I am **found**.
When I'm **up**,
I am **down**.
When I **smile**
I will **frown**.
We're opposites!
When I'm **weak**,
I am **strong**.
When I'm **right**,
I am **wrong**
When I PING
I will **PONG**.

Chorus

Curt Bright

2 Words that end in -ly

Listen, point and say as you repeat these opposite words with feeling!

slowly   quickly   quietly   loudly   happily   angrily   sadly

3 Team game: Guess the word!

Each team gets 4 cards. Write a sentence on each card.
Each sentence must end with a different word that ends in **-ly**.

Walk _____.

Say the alphabet _____.

Laugh _____.

Clap your hands _____.

| Walk sadly. |
| Laugh slowly. |

Each team picks a card and acts out the sentence
as a group.
The other teams try to guess the **-ly** describing words.
They write the word on a piece of paper.
If they guess the correct word, they get 1 point.
Teams will take turns acting out sentences.

4 Sticker activity

| bridge | plane | traffic light |

Read the words. Find the stickers.

Can you think of a word that is the opposite of **bridge**?
Put the stickers on the City page (page 171) of the Picture dictionary.

> 9.6 *City Mouse and Country Mouse*

We are going to...

• **read and discuss a story.**

1 **Making connections**

Some people like the city. Other people like the country. How about you? As you read this story, ask yourself, 'Am I a city mouse or a country mouse?'

City Mouse and Country Mouse

Cindy, the city mouse, and Callie, the country mouse, met on the TV show, *Changing Places*.

'Welcome to *Changing Places*!' said the announcer. 'On this show, you change places for a week.'

Callie had never been to the city. Cindy had never been to the country.

'You'll love the city,' said Cindy. 'There is so much to see and do. There is always something happening.'

'Wow,' said Callie. 'That sounds great. The country is wonderful too. The bees buzz and the birds sing. At night, you can count the stars.'

'That sounds wonderful,' said Cindy.

That evening, Callie arrived in the city. The city streets were full of life. There were shops and cafes, bright lights and music.

Some mice waved to Callie. 'Hi Callie, welcome to the city,' they said. 'We're Cindy's friends. Come to our party.'

The party was at the top of a high building. There was food and dancing.

'This is amazing,' said Callie. 'I love the city.'

'We do, too!' said Cindy's friends.

Just then there was a strange noise. 'What's that?' asked Callie.

'It's a cat,' shouted the other mice. 'Run for your life!'

Callie ran out of the door, down the stairs and into the street. She jumped into a taxi.

'Take me home,' she said. 'The city is too scary for me. I want to go back to the country.'

That same evening, Cindy arrived in the country. Callie's friend Carlos met Cindy at the bus stop.

'Welcome to the country, Cindy,' he said. 'My name is Carlos. Would you like to have a picnic?'

Carlos and Cindy ate fresh berries and nuts. They listened to the birds sing. The sky grew dark and the stars came out.

This is beautiful,' said Cindy. 'I love the country.'

'I do, too!' said Carlos.

Just then Carlos shouted, 'Quickly! Run and hide. Here comes an owl!'

Cindy and Carlos jumped down a mouse hole just in time. The owl flew away.

Cindy hurried to the bus stop. 'Thank you for the picnic, Carlos,' she said. 'But the country is too scary for me. I'm going back to the city.'

That night in the country, Callie said, 'I'm so happy to be home!'

That night in the city, Cindy said, 'I'm so happy to be home!'

2 Talk about it.

a What did Callie like about the city?

b What didn't she like about the city?

c What did Cindy like about the country?

d What didn't she like about the country?

3 Values: East, west, home is best.

What is one thing you love about your home? Share your thoughts with a group of classmates.

4 Write and draw.

Which do you like better, the city or the country? Talk about your answer with a partner. Explain what you like about the city or the country. Plan a trip to the place you like best. What will you do there? Write some sentences. Draw a picture.

I will go to the country.

I will see sheep and lambs.

I will ride a horse.

〉 9.7 Project challenge

Work on the project with a partner or group. Then share with the class.

A: Write a poem about your favourite place

Think about your favourite place. It can be a place in the city, a place in the country or a special place in your home.

- What can you see, hear and do in your favourite place?

- How do you feel when you are there?

- Write a poem and draw a picture. Give your poem a title.

- Make a book of all your poems. Write the title and authors' names on the cover.

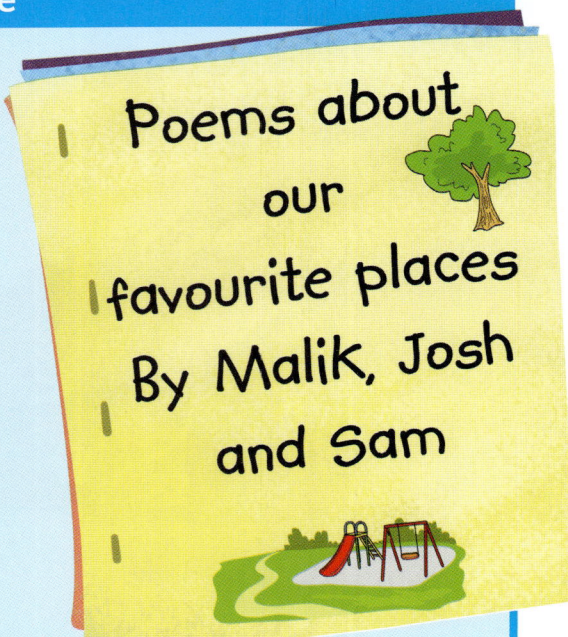

Poems about our favourite places By Malik, Josh and Sam

B: Make your own café

Choose a name for your café.

Make a menu. You can use the computer or use paper and markers.

Act out a conversation at your café. One person can be the waiter and the rest can be customers.

Can I take your order, please?

C: Plan an end-of-school celebration

What will you do to celebrate?

Brainstorm ideas, then make a poster.

Write and draw what you will do at your celebration.

Come to our celebration!

- We will play games.
- We will

What part of this project did you like best?

Look what I can do!

	☹	☺
I can talk about city things and places.	○	○
I can use describing words.	○	○
I can follow and give directions.	○	○
I can talk and write about the past, present and future.	○	○
I can use opposite words.	○	○
I can read and discuss a story.	○	○

> ## Check your progress 3
> # Thinking in **3** s

You need:

- 2 to 3 players
- a different game marker for each player
- number cards.

Directions

- Take a number card.
- Count and move your game marker on the game track.
- Read and answer the questions.
- Read and follow the directions.

16 Say **3** things you did yesterday.

15 Name **3** parts of this plant.

14 Name **3** things you don't see in your classroom.

13 Name **3** things in a house.

12 Spell this **3** letter word.

START

1 Name **3** animals with wings.

2 Name **3** things you are wearing.

3 Spell this **3** letter word.

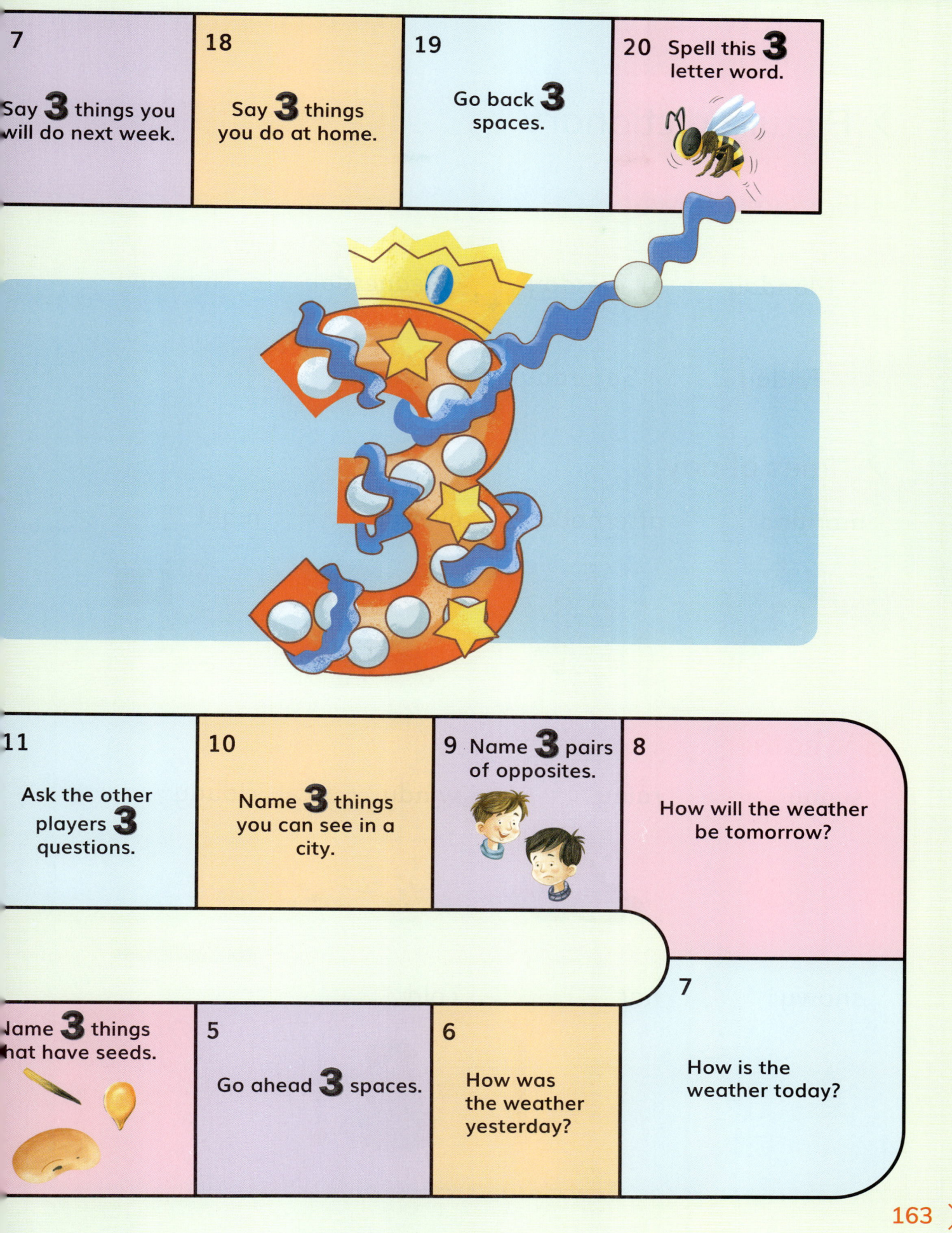

7

Say **3** things you will do next week.

18

Say **3** things you do at home.

19

Go back **3** spaces.

20 Spell this **3** letter word.

11

Ask the other players **3** questions.

10

Name **3** things you can see in a city.

9 Name **3** pairs of opposites.

8

How will the weather be tomorrow?

7

How is the weather today?

Name **3** things that have seeds.

5

Go ahead **3** spaces.

6

How was the weather yesterday?

> Picture dictionary

1 Days of the week

Monday	Tuesday	Wednesday	Thursday

Friday	Saturday	Sunday

2 Times of day

morning   afternoon   evening   night

3 Weather

sunny   rainy   windy   cloudy

snowy   hot   cold

4 The alphabet

Aa apple	**Bb** book	**Cc** cat	**Dd** duck
Ee egg	**Ff** fish	**Gg** guitar	**Hh** hand
Ii insect	**Jj** jacket	**Kk** kite	**Ll** leaf
Mm mouth	**Nn** nine	**Oo** octopus	**Pp** pencil
Qq quilt	**Rr** rain	**Ss** sun	**Tt** table
Uu umbrella	**Vv** violin	**Ww** window	**Xx** box
Yy yellow	**Zz** zoo		

5 Numbers 1–15

1 – one	6 – six	11 – eleven
2 – two	7 – seven	12 – twelve
3 – three	8 – eight	13 – thirteen
4 – four	9 – nine	14 – fourteen
5 – five	10 – ten	15 – fifteen

6 Numbers 15–100

15 – fifteen	20 – twenty	60 – sixty
16 – sixteen	21 – twenty-one	70 – seventy
17 – seventeen	30 – thirty	80 – eighty
18 – eighteen	40 – forty	90 – ninety
19 – nineteen	50 – fifty	100 – one hundred

7 Colours

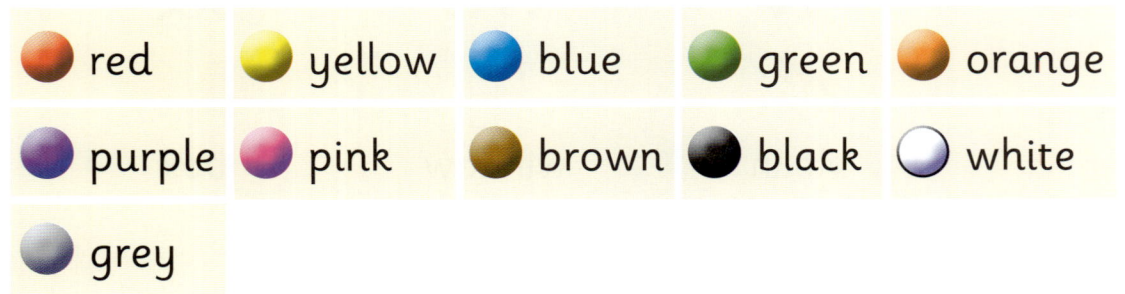

red   yellow   blue   green   orange

purple   pink   brown   black   white

grey

8 The body and clothes

head
hair
eye
ear
mouth
nose
shoulder
chest
elbow
arm
tummy
wrist
hand
fingers
knee
leg
ankle
foot
toes

shoes	sock
hat	skirt
shirt	dress
boots	glasses
jacket	
jumper	
backpack	
trousers	

9 Home

bathroom	bed	bedroom
chair	cooker	cupboard
door	floor	garden
kitchen	lamp	refrigerator
roof	rug	shower
sink	table	toilet
TV	Draw and write.	
window		

10 School

book	bookcase	boy
children	clock	computer
crayons	girl	glue
map	paper	pen
pencil	playground	ruler
scissors	slide	swing
tablet	Draw and write.	
teacher		

11 Food

apple	banana	bread
cake	carrot	cheese
egg	grapes	juice
meat	milk	onion
orange	pear	pizza
potato	rice	sandwich
soup	Draw and write.	
tea		

12 The city

apartment building 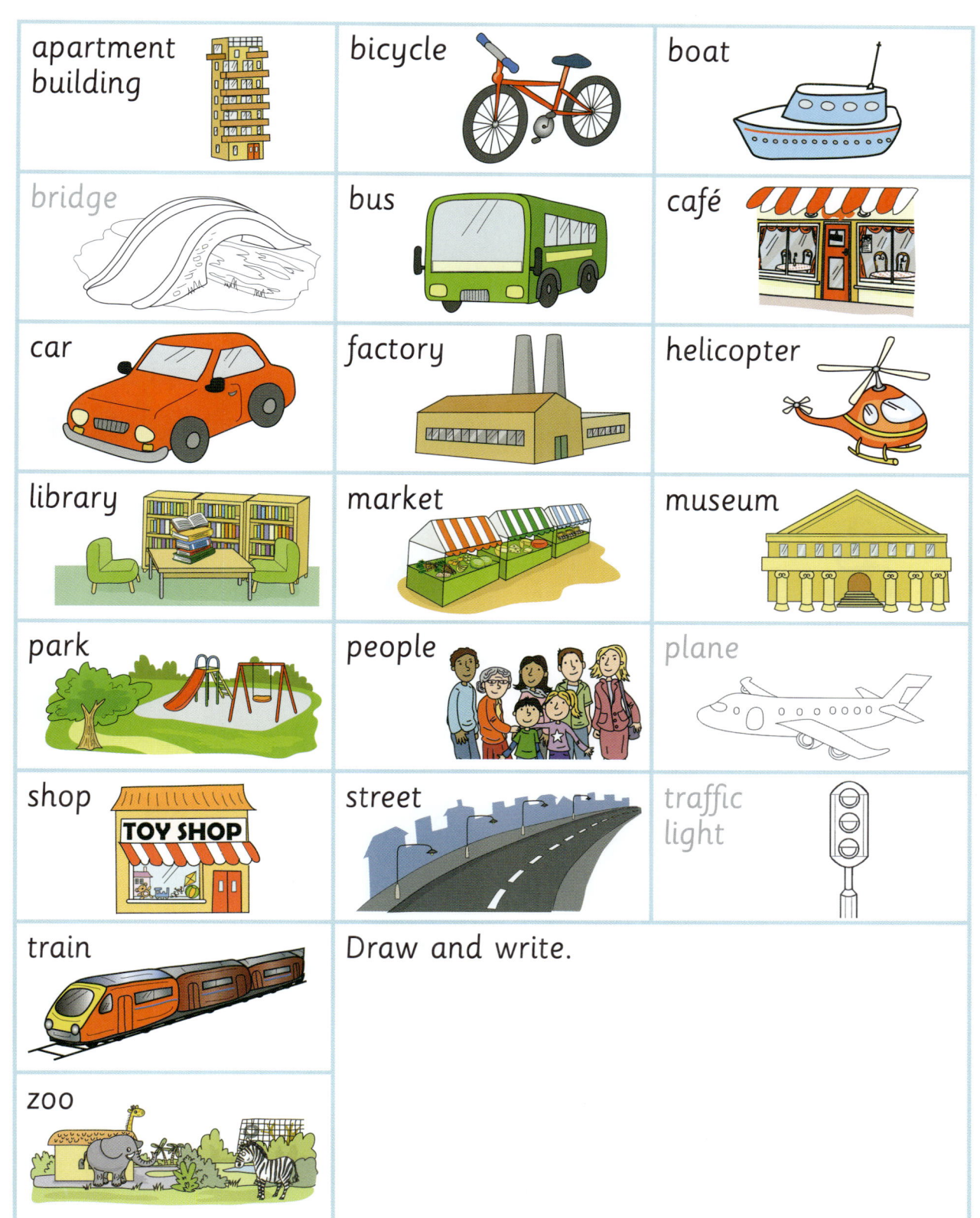	bicycle	boat
bridge	bus	café
car	factory	helicopter
library	market	museum
park	people	plane
shop	street	traffic light
train	Draw and write.	
zoo		

13 Jobs

actor	architect	artist
astronomer	baker	clothes designer
dancer	doctor	farmer
firefighter	football player	musician
nurse	painter	pilot
police officer	scientist	singer
teacher	Draw and write.	
writer		

14 Animals

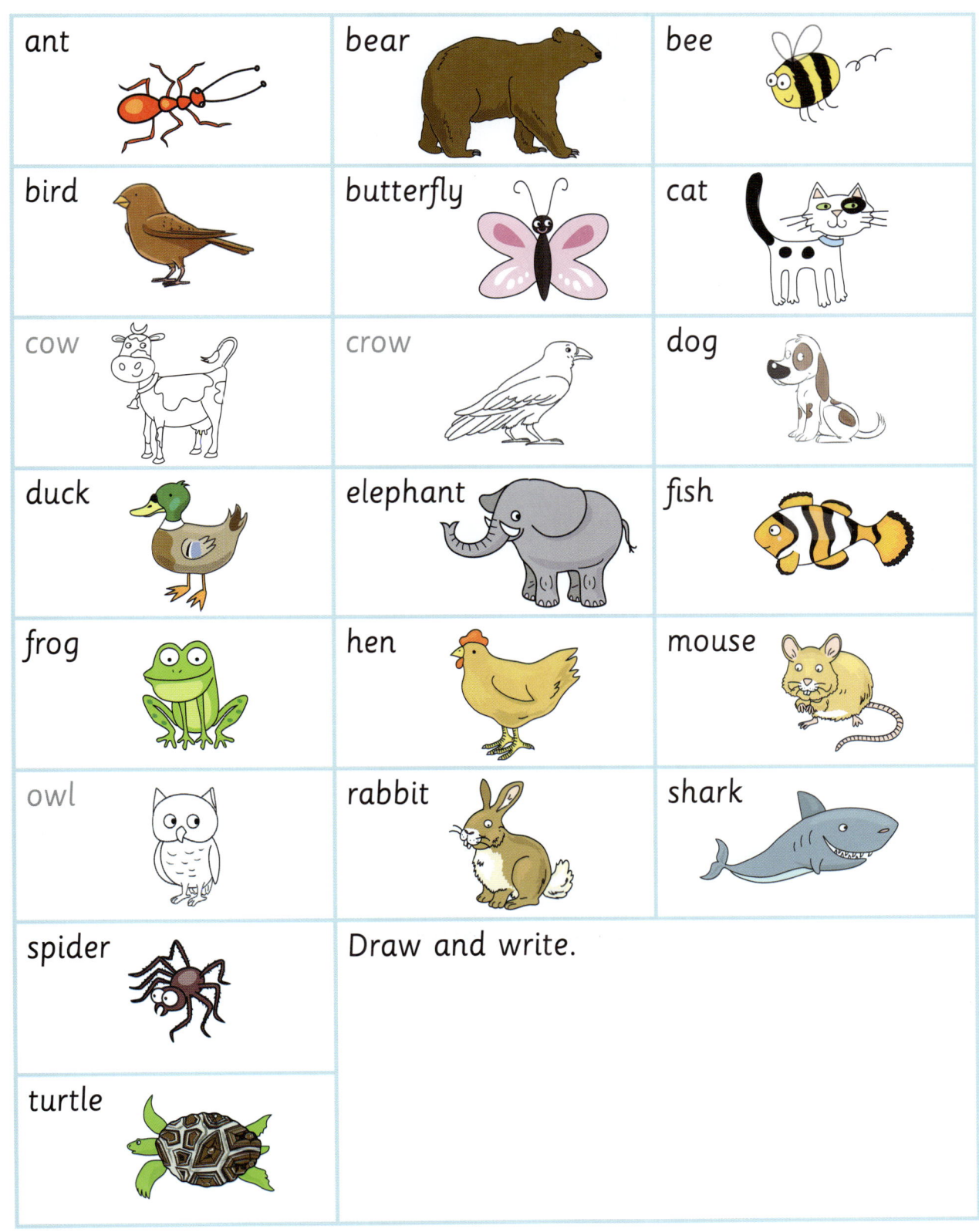

ant	bear	bee
bird	butterfly	cat
cow	crow	dog
duck	elephant	fish
frog	hen	mouse
owl	rabbit	shark
spider	Draw and write.	
turtle		

15 Actions

build (built)	climb	cut (cut)
draw (drew)	eat (ate)	fall (fell)
fly (flew)	jump	measure
play	read (read)	run (ran)
see (saw)	sit (sat)	stand (stood)
swim (swam)	talk	throw (threw)
walk	Draw and write.	
write (wrote)		

16 Nature

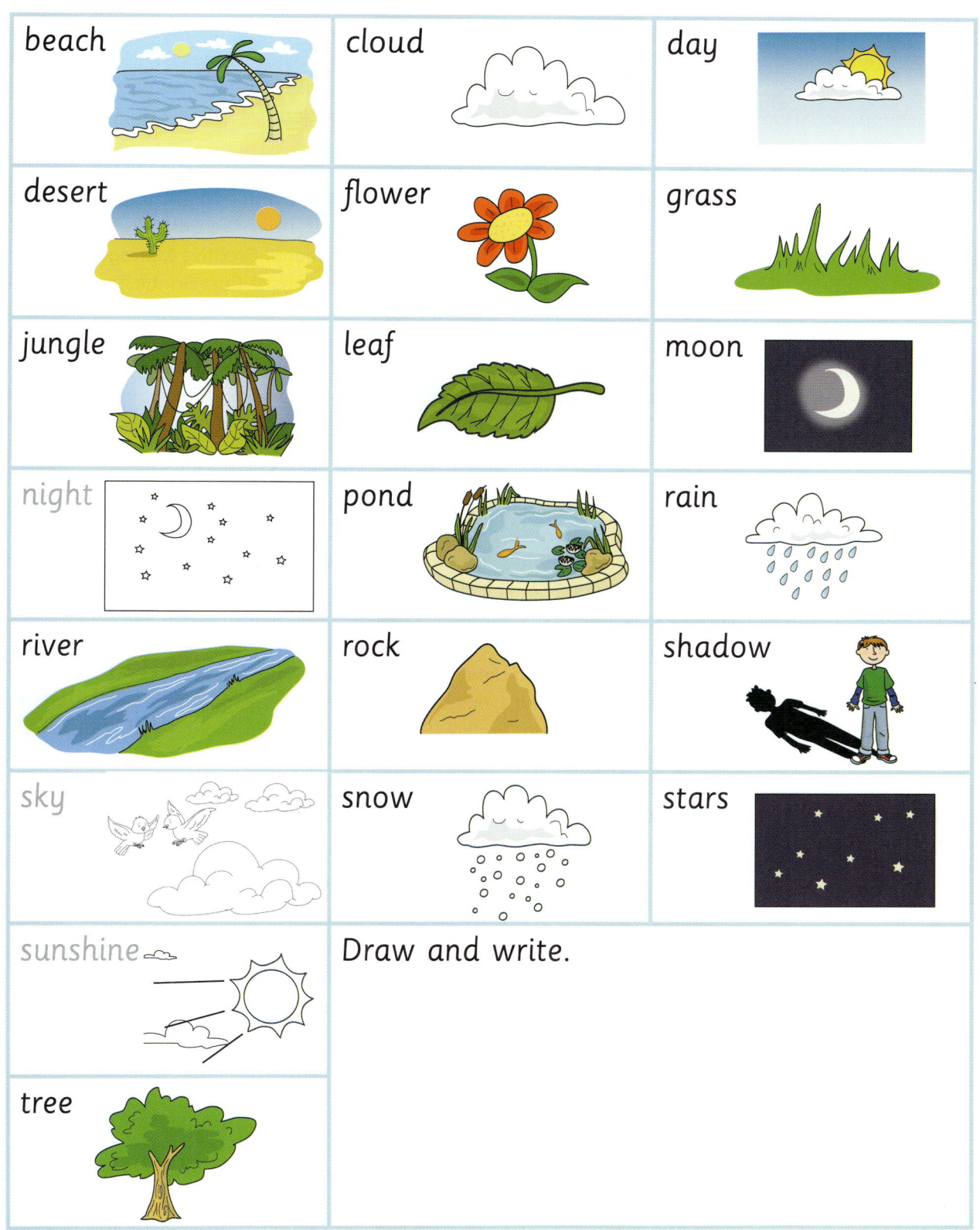

beach

cloud

day

desert

flower

grass

jungle

leaf

moon

night

pond

rain

river

rock

shadow

sky

snow

stars

sunshine

Draw and write.

tree

Acknowledgements

The authors and publishers acknowledge the following sources of copyright material and are grateful for the permissions granted. While every effort has been made, it has not always been possible to identify the sources of all the material used, or to trace all copyright holders. If any omissions are brought to our notice, we will be happy to include the appropriate acknowledgements on reprinting.

The song '12 months in a year' is adapted from *What Month Was Jesus Born In?* © Ludlow Music, Inc. Assigned to TRO Essex Music Limited of Suite 2.07, Plaza 535 Kings Road, London SW10 0SZ International Copyright Secured. All Rights Reserved. Used by Permission; 'A Lot of Kids' from *The Butterfly Jar* by Jeff Moss, copyright © 1989, by Jeff Moss. Reprinted by permission of International Creative Management, Inc.; 'Opposites' written and used by permission of Curt Bright of The String Beans © Curt Bright; Traditional song recordings from *Primary Music Box* © Cambridge University Press

Thanks to the following for permission to reproduce images:
Cover by Omar Aranda (Beehive Illustration); **Unit 1:** ncognet0/GI; Todd Warnock/GI; Rohit Seth/Shutterstock; BJI/GI; ArabianEye/GI; Stuart Fox/GI; Kirill Kukhmar/GI; AtomicCupcake/GI; FatCamera/GI; SDI Productions/GI; Jose Luis Pelaez/GI; Prapass Pulsub/GI; NickS/GI; **Unit 2:** martin-dm/GI; Henry Arden/GI; GoodLifeStudio/GI; Georgette Douwma/GI; Susanne Kronholm/GI; **Unit 3:** Nontawat Thongsibsong/GI; Mike Bons/500px/GI; James Warwick/GI; colibri2003/GI; Randy Green/GI; Ingram Publishing/GI; Grapix/GI; skynesher/GI; Pete Pahham/GI; pkujiahe/GI; emreogan/GI; FatCamera/GI; Christopher Hopefitch/GI; Catherine Falls Commercial/GI; **Unit 4:** Scott Dendy/EyeEm/GI; Sergei Savostyanov/GI; Stephan Dötsch/GI; GettyImages/GI; John Aravosis/GI; Scott Dendy/EyeEm/GI; KTSDesign/Science Photo Library/GI; Pakin Songmor/GI; Caspar Benson/GI; Pakin Songmor/GI; **Unit 5:** JGI/Jamie Grill; Neustockimages/GI; **Unit 6:** Sean Justice/GI; Antrey/GI; Juan Carlos Vindas/GI; Karthik Photography/GI; Nachteule/GI; Soteavy Som/EyeEm/GI; sofiaworld/GI; Rodrigo Albano/GI; AlpamayoPhoto/GI; zaricm/GI; **Unit 7:** FingerMedium/GI; Andreas Herrmann/GI; Jose Luis Pelaez Inc/GI; skodonnell/GI; Jeff Greenberg/GI; Albasir Canizares/GI; miodrag ignjatovic/GI; izzetugutmen/GI; Sungmoon Han/GI; Micheline Pelletier/GI; **Unit 8:** Jose A. Bernat Bacete; S. Greg Panosian/GI; Mohd Firdaus Haron/GI; Cappadocia/GI; Anastasios71/Shutterstock; Alan Powdrill/GI; Matthew Horwood/GI; koosen/GI; venakr/GI; pioneer111/GI; imanolurquizu/GI; Carlos Ciudad Photography/GI; CreativeNature_nl/GI; Jose A. Bernat Bacete/GI; smuay/GI; Danita Delimont; Antrey/GI; AlasdairJames/GI; richcarey/GI; Life On White/GI; GlobalP/GI; GlobalP/GI; **Unit 9:** exxorian/GI; Kat Chadwick/GI

GI = Getty Images

Stickers for Unit 1 page 16

We draw.

We write.

We sing.

We play.

We read.

Stickers for Unit 2 page 32

 helmet

 jacket

 boots

 gloves

 mask

Stickers for Unit 3 page 48

hop

touch

clap

stand

wave

Stickers for Unit 4 page 66

Stickers for Unit 5 page 82

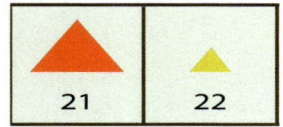  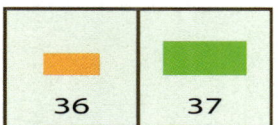 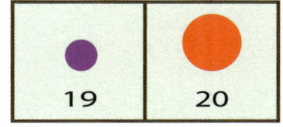

Stickers for Unit 6 page 98

 ant  bee  butterfly

 worm  cricket  spider

Stickers for Unit 7 page 116

 roots stem  leaf

 flower

Stickers for Unit 8 page 132

bed

sink

toilet

Stickers for Unit 9 page 148

octopus

jellyfish

penguin

sea turtle

Stickers for Picture dictionary Unit 1 page 22

Aa

apple

Ee

egg

Ii

insect

Oo

octopus

Uu

umbrella

Stickers for Picture dictionary Unit 2 page 39

actor

baker

doctor

nurse

painter

Stickers for Picture dictionary Unit 3 page 55

glue

playground

slide

teacher

Stickers for Picture dictionary Unit 4 page 72

night    sky    sunshine

Stickers for Picture dictionary Unit 5 page 88

1 – one	2 – two
4 – four	8 – eight

Stickers for Picture dictionary Unit 6 page 105

bread    cheese

meat    tea

Stickers for Picture dictionary Unit 7 page 123

owl    crow    cow

Stickers for Picture dictionary Unit 8 page 139

roof

bedroom

cooker

Stickers for Picture dictionary Unit 9 page 155

bridge

plane

traffic light